Easter ISLAND

Guide For Inquisitive Minds

Brien Foerster

Easter Island:

Guide For Inquisitive Minds

Copyright Brien Foerster 2013

Cover by Hans Messershmidt

Disclaimer: All of the content of this book was gleaned from information by other authors, internet sources and personal observations by me during two visits to Rapa Nui (Easter Island) as well as from local informants on the island. Also, all photos were either taken by me, the author, or were found on what are presumed to be copyright free websites. Any use of written or visual material which is not copyright free was completely unintentional.

I in no way believe that this is the definitive book on the subject of Easter Island, but it is an attempt to present a balanced thesis. The only people, in my opinion, that are the true experts of the history of this place are the Native residents, the Rapa Nui, but as far as I know, at this time, none have written a book on the subject.

Should such a text appear, I will readily wish to read the contents...

My biography, other books, media appearances and guided tours can be found at:

www.hiddenincatours.com

Hans Messerschmidt, the brilliant designer of the cover can be contacted at:

hans@themodcorp.com

And his website is: **www.themodcorp.com**

Chapters

1/ Introduction

2/ What Is In A Name?

3/ Evidence Of Two Distinct Cultures

4/ Ancient Connections With South America?

5/ When Was The Island First Settled?

6/ The Ahu And Moai

7/ Population Decline And Ecocide

8/ Making The Moai Walk

9/ Pukao: Red Hair Or Red Hats?

10/ Rongorongo: The Only Polynesian Text?

11/ Non Polynesian DNA Prior To Europeans?

The Important Sites:

12/ Ahu Vinapu

13/ Orongo

14/ Rano Raraku

15/ Ahu Tongariki

16/ Ahu Tahai

17/ Puna Pau

18/ Anakena

19/ Ahu Te Pito Kura

20/ Ahu Akivi

1/ Introduction

Of all of the mysterious places on the planet, and especially of the islands inhabited by people for centuries if not for millennia, Easter Island is one that has captured my imagination and that of many other people since childhood. The most striking features of the island are of course are the huge carved stone heads which scatter the landscape, and of which little is truly understood in mainstream anthropology and archaeology, and far less by the general public.

Ideas that aliens made them, that people who worshipped or even were descended from aliens produced them, that they are remnants of a lost ancient civilization, or the idols of ancestors are common speculations, but what are the facts? Combining the knowledge from both archaeology, and Native oral traditions may provide a logical answer...

The author with Rapa Nui elder, Sr. Jorge, who gave me the head adornment

2/ What Is In A Name?

Easter Island sits 3500 km west of the Chilean coast of South America, and is also known as Isla de Pascua (Spanish) and Rapa Nui (the Indigenous language.) This remote outpost of civilization has fascinated visitors ever since it was first discovered by the Dutch explorer Jakob Roggeveen on Easter Sunday, 1722; he thus named it Easter Island, or more properly *Paasch-Eyland* (18th century Dutch for "Easter Island.") (1) .That name has stuck ever since, much to the consternation of the Native islanders, who have known their home by their own names for hundreds if not thousands of years.

The name Rapa Nui, for example, which is the title best loved by the present day population, who are a mix of Polynesian and Chilean descent, means "Big Rapa," but this term was supposedly coined after the slave raids of the early 1860s, and refers to the island's topographic resemblance to the island of Rapa in the Bass

Islands of the Austral Islands group. (2) In the source's own words, he being William Thompson writing in 1891, 'Throughout southeastern Polynesia this island is known as Rapa Nui, but the name is of accidental origin and only traces back about twenty years. When the islanders, kidnapped by the Peruvians, were being returned to their homes, there was for a time a question as to the identity of those from Easter Island. The native name of "Te Pito O Te Henua" was not recognized by the French officials, and finding certain fellow-sufferers hailing from Oparo, an island lying 2,000 miles to the westward, were more successful under the local appellation of Rapa Iti (Little Rapa), the euphonious title was dropped and Rapa nui (Great Rapa) substituted.'

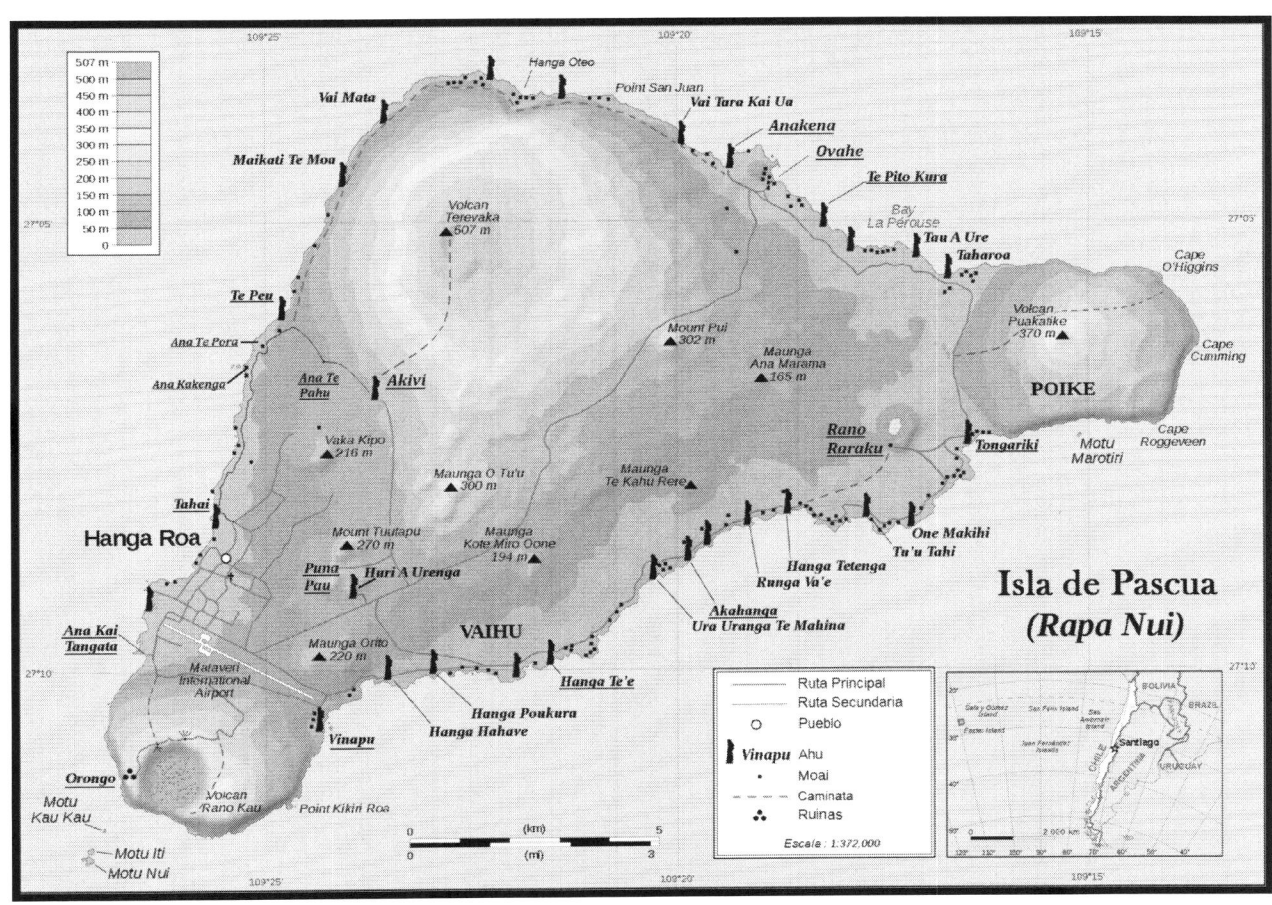

Map of Rapa Nui (Easter Island)

Te Pito O te Henua has been said to be the original title of the island since Alphonse Pinart gave it the romantic translation "The Navel Of The World" in his Voyage à l'Île de Pâques, published in 1877. (3) However, there are two words pronounced pito in Rapa Nui, one meaning 'navel' and one 'end', and the phrase can thus also mean "land's end".

Yet another name, that being Mata Ki Te Rangi, means "Eyes Looking To The Sky" and this may be in reference to the famous large stone statues, called Moai, which ring the island and are in the shape of, predominantly, human heads and torsos. At least that is the western interpretation of the name and phrase, whereas local informants have told me that the Moai look towards the villages and descendants, and not the sky. However, after my second trip there in November of 2012, I tend to believe that at least some of the Moai were made such that their eyes are truly looking skywards, on purpose. And finally, Thor Heyerdahl, the amazing Norwegian explorer best known for his 1947 Kon Tiki adventure, and later the Ra and Tigris expeditions, insisted that Rapa was the original name of Easter Island, and that Rapa Iti was named by refugees from there. (4) Heyerdahl was in fact the first European, and in fact outsider, to conduct archaeological excavations on the island, which is well documented in his book Aku Aku: the Secret of Easter Island written in 1958.

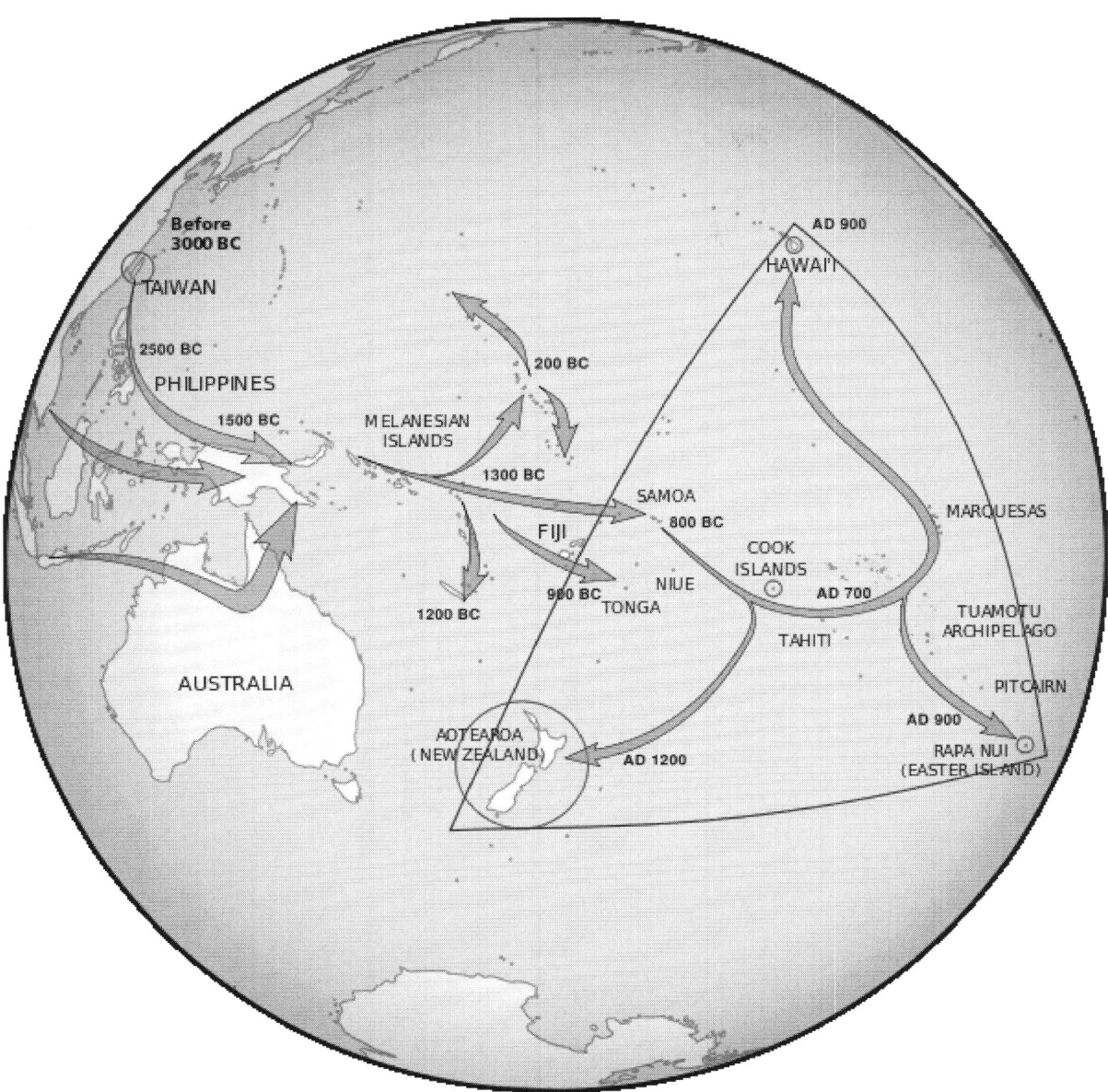

Conventional archaeological map of the migration of "Polynesian" people

Cover of Aku-Aku, no longer in print

3/ Evidence Of Two Distinct Cultures

Francis Mazière, who conducted archaeological excavations on the island in 1963, was told by a native elder that 'very big men, but not giants, lived on the island well before the coming of Hotu Matu'a (the presumed Polynesian founder of the island.) Another related the following legend:

The first men to live on the island were the survivors of the world's first race. They were yellow, very big, with long arms, great stout chests, huge ears although their lobes were not stretched: they had pure yellow hair and their bodies were hairless and shining. They did not possess fire. This race once existed on two other Polynesian islands. They came by boat from a land that lies behind America.

What is perhaps most intriguing and perplexing about Rapa Nui are the recurring stories of two separate people and cultures cohabiting this small place which Roggeveen was the first outsider to witness in 1722. He states that they were "of all shades of colour, yellow, white and brown" and they distended their ear lobes so greatly with large disks that when they took them out they could "hitch the rim of the lobe over the top of the ear". (5) The latter is in reference to the so-called Long Ears, or Hanau e'epe people, who are generally regarded as having been a high caste group, whereas the Hanau momoko were the Short Ears, and the working class.

Long Ears: these with the distinctive top knots

The Hanau e'epe were theorized by Thor Heyerdahl to have come from South America (6), perhaps being the early Inca or the predecessors, while the Hanau momoko were Polynesians, most likely coming from Oparo or Rapa Iti Island which is in the Australs. Much controversy surrounds the relationships between these people, as well as time lines of conflicts that in fact did occur; however, a full discussion of this will come later. Roggeveen clearly indicated that he observed two distinct peoples upon his arrival to Easter Island, the Polynesians, and "White" people, whose ear lobes were heavily distended. Not only was their skin colour much lighter than the Polynesians or Hanau momoko, but their hair was also reddish or even blonde. Such hair is depicted in the above photo of the Moai wearing top knots called Pukao.

Enigmatic possible megalithic remains on Rapa Iti

What Heyerdahl purports in Aku Aku is that the evidence exists to show that the island was "invaded" by a white skinned people that arrived on the island about 500 A.D. This race of people had unusual features that included red hair and long thin noses. They were remembered by the natives as the "Long Ears" because they wore large ear rings that elongated their earlobes. They took possession of the island and forced the natives to work as labourers. Descendants of the Long Ears are said to still exist on the island today, though in my travels I never saw a person whose ears were physically that abnormal. They are believed by some western researchers to be predominant families, many of them still with red hair and European facial features that set them apart from the dark haired, dark-eyed natives. (7)

Great disputes arise in the timing and identity of these two groups, the Hanau e'epe (Long Ears) and Hanau momoko (Short Ears.) Conventional wisdom, taken from the loosest of sources, as in Wikipedia, tells us the following: estimated dates of the initial settlement of Easter Island range from 300 to 1200 CE, approximately coinciding with the arrival of the first settlers in Hawaii. Rectifications in radiocarbon dating have changed almost all of the previously-posited early settlement dates in Polynesia. Rapa Nui is now considered to have been settled about 700–1100 CE. An ongoing study by archaeologists Terry Hunt and Carl Lipo suggests a still–later date: "Radiocarbon dates for the earliest stratigraphic layers at Anakena, Easter Island, and analysis of previous radiocarbon dates imply that the island was colonized late, about 1200 CE. Significant ecological impacts and major cultural investments in monumental architecture and statuary thus began soon after initial settlement." (8)

However, such a broad range of dates, even with radiocarbon as a time measure more clutters the situation than defines it, when, again, taking into account the two separate groups that dwelt there, and the Native oral traditions of the Rapa Nui people.

According to Thor Heyerdahl's own words, delivered in a series of lectures to the Swedish Society of Anthropology and Geography in Stockholm: "at some unidentified date prior to AD 380, the first settlers landed on Easter Island, and found a verdant island covered by trees, shrubs, and palms." He proved this to be true from the extensive pollen samples taken from the crater lakes with the aid of 26 feet long cores from the sediments.

His excavations proved that there were 3 separate epochs in the History of Easter Island, which the archaeologists have named Early, Middle and Late Periods. In the Early Period there was no production of giant statues, only altar-like elevations of very large, and most precisely cut and joined stones, which were erected with their facades towards the ocean, and a sunken court on the inland side. They were astronomically oriented, and constructed by highly specialised stone masons who studied the annual movement of the sun and in their religious architecture.

The author at the megalithic walled platform of Vinapu

Not until the Second Period were the well known giant statues, the Moai quarried and placed on the platforms. Some archaeologists believe that during this period, around AD 1100, the Birdman Cult arrived and marked the commencement of the raising of the large ancestor statues. During a period of less than 6 centuries, more than 600 giant ancestor statues were carved from the quarries on the slopes of Rano Raraku crater after the forests had been cleared. When the statue production reached its peak the island engineers were able to erect statues up to 40 feet tall, weighing more than 80 tons, and balance a red stone cylinder hat, the Pukao weighing up to 12 tons, on top of its head.

According again to Heyerdahl, about 50 years after Roggeveen first visited Rapa Nui, the Spaniard Don Felipe Gonzales was the next foreigner to describe the people of this island, in 1770. "The Spaniards met on the island tall, fair men. Two of the biggest were measured and were respectively 6 feet, 6 l/2 inches and 6 feet, 5 inches tall. Many had beards, and the Spaniards found that they were quite like Europeans and not ordinary natives. They noted in their diaries that not all of them had black hair: the hair of some was chestnut brown, and in other cases it was even reddish and cinnamon-colored." (9)

Auburn haired resident of Rapa Nui

4/ Ancient Connections With South America?

'Polynesian archaeology appears to be dominated by a small, zealous group, who will not permit any points of view other than their own. ... We must bear in mind that nobody, absolutely nobody has the right to claim to know the whole truth about the past; for there are simply too many elements of uncertainty involved.' Øystein Kock Johansen (9a)

Thor Heyerdahl, who led archaeological expeditions to Easter Island in 1955-56 and 1986-88, opposed the conventional view that Easter Island was first peopled from the west (Polynesia), and argued that it was first settled from the east (South America), as one of the island's early traditions suggests. He held that the sweet potato, bottle gourd, and totora reed were introduced to the island from South America, while the chicken, banana, and sugar cane, for example, were introduced from Polynesia.

Most researchers dismiss Heyerdahl's theory of a South American source for Easter Island's culture, arguing that not a single South American artifact has ever been found in 50 years of intensive archaeology in Polynesia, and that there is no trace of a sudden influx of new cultural influences at any point in Easter Island's history. They describe his theory as 'a tottering edifice precariously based on preconceptions, extreme subjectivity, distortions and very little hard evidence'. (9b)

They do, however, concede that there must have been at least sporadic contacts between Polynesians and South America, though they think it was probably the Polynesians who went to South America rather than the other way round.

Contacts of some kind are needed to explain how the sweet potato, for example, reached Polynesia, and why the Inca quipu, a system of knotted cords for remembering facts and especially numbers is used on many island in Polynesia and Melanesia, into Indonesia and through China. There is archaeological and linguistic evidence that Polynesians landed on the north coast of Chile, among a tribe known as the Mapuche. In graves at Rio Negro in Argentina, human remains have been found that do not belong to any race of South America, but to those of

Polynesia. Maori stone implements have been discovered at Cuzco in Peru and at Santiago del Estiro in Argentina. Carved wooden clubs similar to those of the Marquesas have been found in Peru, Chile, Columbia, and Ecuador. (9c)

The official thinking today is that the ancestral Easter Islanders were Polynesians, with no admixture of any other groups. However, the 'scientific' evidence is ambiguous. H.L. Shapiro found that Easter Islanders deviated significantly from the Polynesians in the shape and dimensions of the cranium, but proposed that this might be due to 'selective migration followed by isolation and inbreeding'; the Easter Islanders have been said to be just plain Polynesians of 'a somewhat specialized and exaggerated type'. (9d)

The rocker jaw is the most characteristically Polynesian skeletal trait. Its frequency of occurrence on almost all islands from New Zealand to Hawaii ranges from 72 to 90%, but it is extremely rare among Amerindians; the figure for Easter Island is 48.5%. One researcher found that the Easter Islanders show a few minor Amerindian traits, and suggested this could be due to some Marquesans having sailed to South America. (9e)

Thor Heyerdahl based his theory of emigration from South America in large part on the oral traditions of the people of the Peruvian and Bolivian highlands, especially around Lake Titicaca, which spoke of the characters known as Kon Tiki and Viracocha. Most scholars agree that these two characters were one and the same, and in fact another interpretation of the name is Con Ticci Viracocha.

The Viracocha symbol as used on the Kon Tiki raft

According to "History of the Incas" by Pedro Sarmiento De Gamboa, "The natives of this land affirm that in the beginning, and before this world was created, there was a being called Viracocha. He created a dark world without sun, moon or stars.

Owing to this creation he was named Viracocha Pachayachachi, which means "Creator of all things." And when he had created the world he formed a race of giants of disproportioned greatness painted and sculptured, to see whether it would be well to make real men of that size. He then created men in his likeness as they are now; and they lived in darkness."

Image of Viracocha on the Sun Gate at Tiwanaku Bolivia

"Viracocha ordered these people that they should live without quarrelling, and that they should know and serve him." As men became bad, he decided to punish them; he turned them into stone, into things, and some were swallowed up by the earth and others by the sea. A general flood which they call Uñu Pachacuti, meaning "water that overturns the land", came over them. "They say that it rained 60 days and nights, that it drowned all created things, and that there alone remained some vestiges of those who were turned into stones, as a memorial of the event, and as an example to posterity, in the edifices of Pucara, which are 60 leagues from Cuzco."

"He lived amongst men, and he taught them many arts. He it was, as the priests of those who were here before the Incas say, showed men how to bring streams of water to their crops, and taught them how to build terraces upon the mountains where crops would grow. And when the bird that cries out four times at dawn cried out, and the light came upon the cross he had set up, Viracocha went from amongst men. He went down to the sea, and he walked across it towards the west. But he told those whom he had left behind that he would send messengers back who would protect them and give them renewed knowledge of all he had taught them." (10)

The timeline of Viracocha's exit from the mainland of South America, the departure point most often believed having been northern Peru in the area of the present town of Tumbes, is completely unknown, lost in the fog of time. However, it would have been prior to the existence of the Inca, which most accounts give as beginning about the year 900 AD, when they were forced to leave the Tiwanaku area, near lake Titicaca in Bolivia, and found Cusco, which was to become their capital city. (11)

Here again Heyerdahl comes into play, not in the 10th century, but the 20th. It was his belief, of course, that at least some of the ancestry of Rapa Nui came from the Pacific side of the South American continent, based on the presence of the clearly non-Polynesian Long Ears, but also on many other factors. The idea that Viracocha, or the Viracochas as a people left the shores of northern Peru on some sort of vessel led Heyerdahl to speculate as to what sort of vessel would have been employed, and where it would have gone.

Thor Heyerdahl and his crew aboard Kon Tiki

Thus arose his building and sailing of the famous Kon Tiki, a balsa wood raft equipped with a large square rigged sail, which he and 5 others crewed from the port of Callao, near Lima Peru. After a 101 day, 4,300-mile (6,900 km) journey across the Pacific Ocean, Kon-Tiki smashed into the reef at Raroia in the Tuamotu Islands on August 7, 1947.

Kon Tiki demonstrated that it was possible for a simple raft to sail the Pacific with relative ease and safety, especially to the west (with the wind and ocean currents). The raft proved to be highly manoeuvrable, and fish congregated between the nine balsa logs in such numbers that ancient sailors could have possibly relied on fish for hydration in the absence of other sources of fresh water. Inspired by Kon Tiki, other rafts have repeated the voyage.

One key factor in the path the raft took was that Heyerdahl and his companions, although they carried some modern navigational aids, and had equipped the Kon Tiki with 5 centreboards and a large aft fixed steering paddle, did not attempt to pre-determine an exact course. They knew that Tahiti, the Marquesas Islands and Tuamotus lay to the west, and that by making their use of the prevailing wind as efficient as possible, would land somewhere amongst one of these island groups.

During the ocean voyage a few experiments were carried out with the centreboards. It was found that the five centreboards, six feet deep and two feet wide, when securely attached, were enough to permit the raft to sail almost at right angles to the wind. It was also ascertained that by raising or lowering the centreboard fore or aft, the raft could be steered without using the steering oar. On this expedition an attempt to tack into the wind failed completely. In 1953 Thor Heyerdahl experimented on a smaller test raft constructed like the Kon Tiki of nine Balsa logs lashed together. He found that a correct interplay between the handling of the sail and the centreboards enabled him to tack against contrary wind, and even to sail back to the exact spot from where he had set off. The centreboard method of steering a raft was astonishing through its simplicity and effectiveness. (12)

These experiments proved that the early Peruvian high cultures were very advanced in marine matters, and that an entire reappraisal of early Peruvian seamanship and navigation was necessary.

None of this is really surprising because in 1748 two Spanish naval officers became sufficiently intrigued by the navigation technique employed by the local Indians to look further into the history of the indigenous centreboards. Part of their report read as follows:

"Hitherto we have only mentioned the construction and the uses they [the raft] are applied to, but the greatest singularity of the floating vessel is that it sails, tacks and works as well in contrary winds as ships with a keel, and makes very little leeway. This advantage it derives from another method of steering than by a rudder, namely, by some boards three or four yards in length, and half a yard in breadth, called guaras, which are placed vertically, both at the head and stern between the main beams. By thrusting some of these deep in the water, and raising others, they bear away, luff up, tack, lay to, and perform all the other motions of a regular ship. The method of steering by these centreboards is so simple, that once a Balsa is put in her proper course, one only has to raise or lower as occasions require, to keep the Balsa in her intended direction."

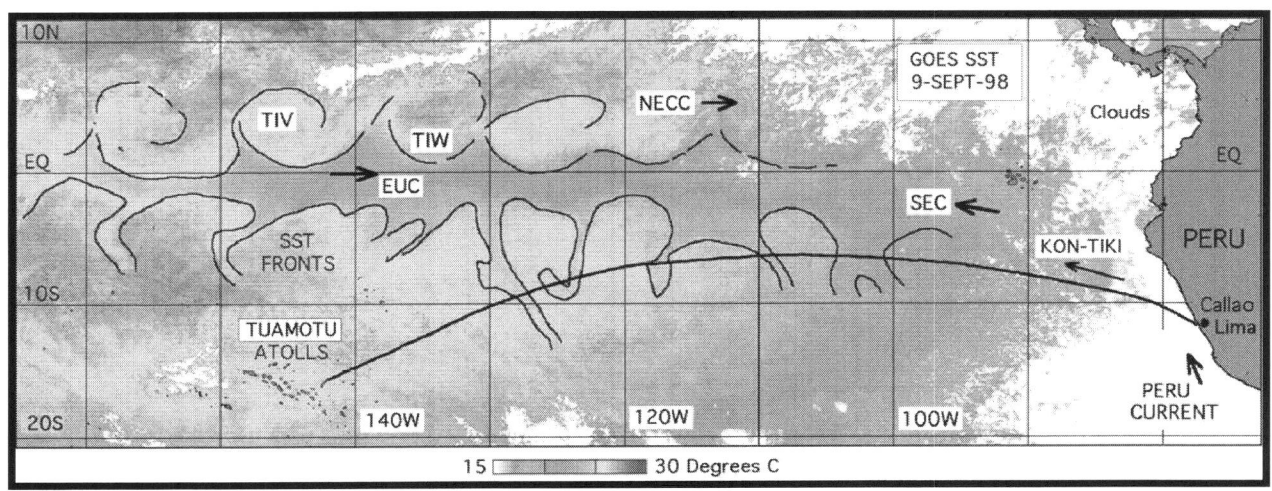

Reconstructed map of the path of the Kon Tiki

Had Heyerdahl and his crew chosen to specifically aim the Kon Tiki to Rapa Nui, it is possible that they could have achieved such a goal, depending on their navigational capabilities and the patterns of the winds and currents at that time. The Humboldt Current, also known as the Peru Current, is a cold, low-salinity ocean current that flows north-westward along the west coast of South America from the southern tip of Chile to northern Peru. It is an eastern boundary current flowing in the direction of the equator, and can extend 1,000 kilometres offshore. It is this current, and prevailing southerly winds which accompany it, that carried the Kon Tiki first northwards and then westwards for its 101 day journey. The presence of El Nino and El Nina events off the shore of Peru, where the offshore water either warms significantly (El Nino) or cools (El Nina) can drastically affect the course of the Humboldt Current. In some cases they would assist in guiding a vessel to Rapa Nui, and in other cases prohibit it.

By the spring of 1997, half a century after the original Kon Tiki expedition, no primitive experimental raft had made the connection between South America and that continent's closest Polynesian island, Easter Island, although Eric de Bisschop had come close in Tahiti-Nui I in 1957, and Kitin Muñoz had drifted on Uru from Peru to the Marquesas in 1988. Heyerdahl's massive ethnological tome "American Indians in the Pacific" had compiled a much greater case for prehistoric reed boat—as opposed to balsa raft—voyages to Easter Island, yet despite the Ra expeditions no one could say from actual experience whether such an expedition was possible.

Such an experimental raft expeditions would connect the reed boat builders of the pre-Inca highlands of Peru with the Pacific ports that could have made use of large versions of lake reed boats. It would connect a potential prehistoric South American port with the most likely Polynesian island to have received cultural impulses from pre-Incan Peru. It would offer a plausible escape route for the legendary prehistoric figure Viracocha, as he fled from the shores of the great highland lake at Titicaca to his exile somewhere toward the setting sun. And it would offer some comparative strength to Heyerdahl's hypothesis that pre-Incan Moche mariners forced to sea during cultural catastrophes triggered by El Niño events would be pushed southwest toward Easter Island.

In 1998, such an experiment was created. Phil Buck, a highly-accomplished mountaineer, announced that he would circumnavigate the globe in a series of five reed boats. The reed ships would all be named for the bearded sun-god Viracocha. The first leg of this enormous undertaking would take the Viracocha I from Arica, a Chilean port near the border with Peru, to Easter Island.

In the late 1998, Buck journeyed to Huatajata, Bolivia, on the shores of Lake Titicaca. There, both the Catari and Limarchi families—many of whom had helped Heyerdahl construct the reed ships Ra II and Tigris—collaborated with Buck to build the hull of Viracocha I. The hull was completed in March of 1999, then stored under a tin roof until it was trucked to the coast in December. During the storage period Buck had the boat builders haul on the hull's ropes each month. Eventually, he considered that this simple step might have been critical to the success of his voyage. Reeds shrink as they dry, and having a solid reed boat is imperative to lower water absorption and lessen the overall flexing of the boat at sea.

The hull was trucked to Arica, Chile, in December 1999, where it was fitted out with masts and sails, rudder oars, and a bamboo cabin. Like Heyerdahl, Buck selected a multi-national crew, in this case three Chileans, a Bolivian, a British, a Frenchman, and one other American. Buck envisioned a six-week expedition to Easter Island, one that would start around January 15 in the new millennium, and reach Easter Island in early March. There the explorers would tramp the island, look in on the totora reeds of the island's crater lakes, and seek permissions for the second leg in the global circumnavigation, from Easter Island to Australia. In the end, Buck's timetable evolved with almost clock-like precision. (13)

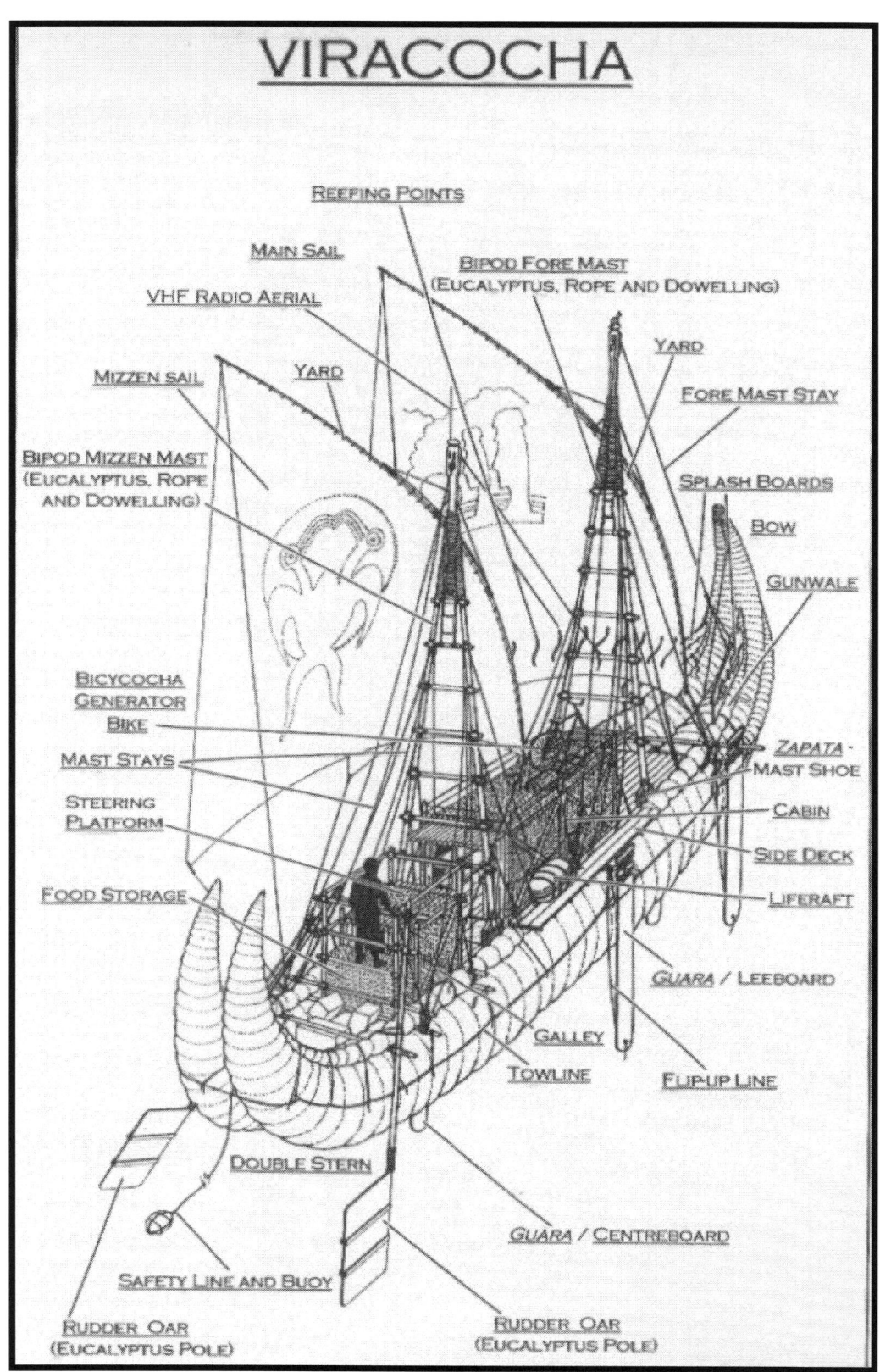

Drawing of the Viracocha I

Viracocha I left Arica on February 25, 2000, after having been placed in the water fifteen days earlier. Norman Baker had suggested to Buck that the raft should be put into the ocean three days prior to departure, to allow the reeds to absorb seawater as ballast, but problems with inspections and computer software delayed the departure.

Three days after leaving the Chilean coast, the reed boat was 150 miles to sea, sailing 150 degrees off the wind and about two knots an hour, on a southwest course toward Easter Island. Over the course of the next forty-four days, the reed boat continued to average about two knots an hour, or about fifty miles a day. On only two or three days did the boat's performance increase or decrease dramatically. On March 9, contrary winds stalled the boat's progress to nothing, while on March 23rd and 26th, the boat skimmed along with the wind at speeds of five and six knots.

By April 1st, 2000, the Viracocha I had sailed more than 2,000 miles from the coast of Chile, and was only 300 miles from Easter Island. As he neared the island of Sala Y Gomez, an uninhabited island 240 miles from Easter Island, the raft began to experience major wind shifts and velocity drops. The winds began to move in a counter-clockwise direction and at time would completely drop off. It was in stark contrast to what Buck had experienced during the first month at sea, when he had steady trade winds from the South and South-East. The raft drifted on calm seas six miles from Sala y Gomez. Buck was now within a long stone's throw of an island Heyerdahl landed on in 1956. He was well aware of the significance of his achievement:

"I thought that passing near Sala Y Gomez was important to Thor Heyerdahl's theories because passing an uninhabited, rocky bird island was one of things that the Spanish Chronicler Sarmiento had heard that Inca and Pre-Incan voyages would pass one week before reaching the island Thor Heyerdahl believes to be Easter Island" (ibid.).

Buck hoped to zero in on the harbor at Anakena, the port on the northeast corner of Easter Island where legends place the arrival of Hotu Matua, the prehistoric maritime explorer and founder of Easter Island culture. As the island emerged out of the Pacific a week later, Buck steered the reed boat around the southern side of the island, to a landing at Hango Piko.

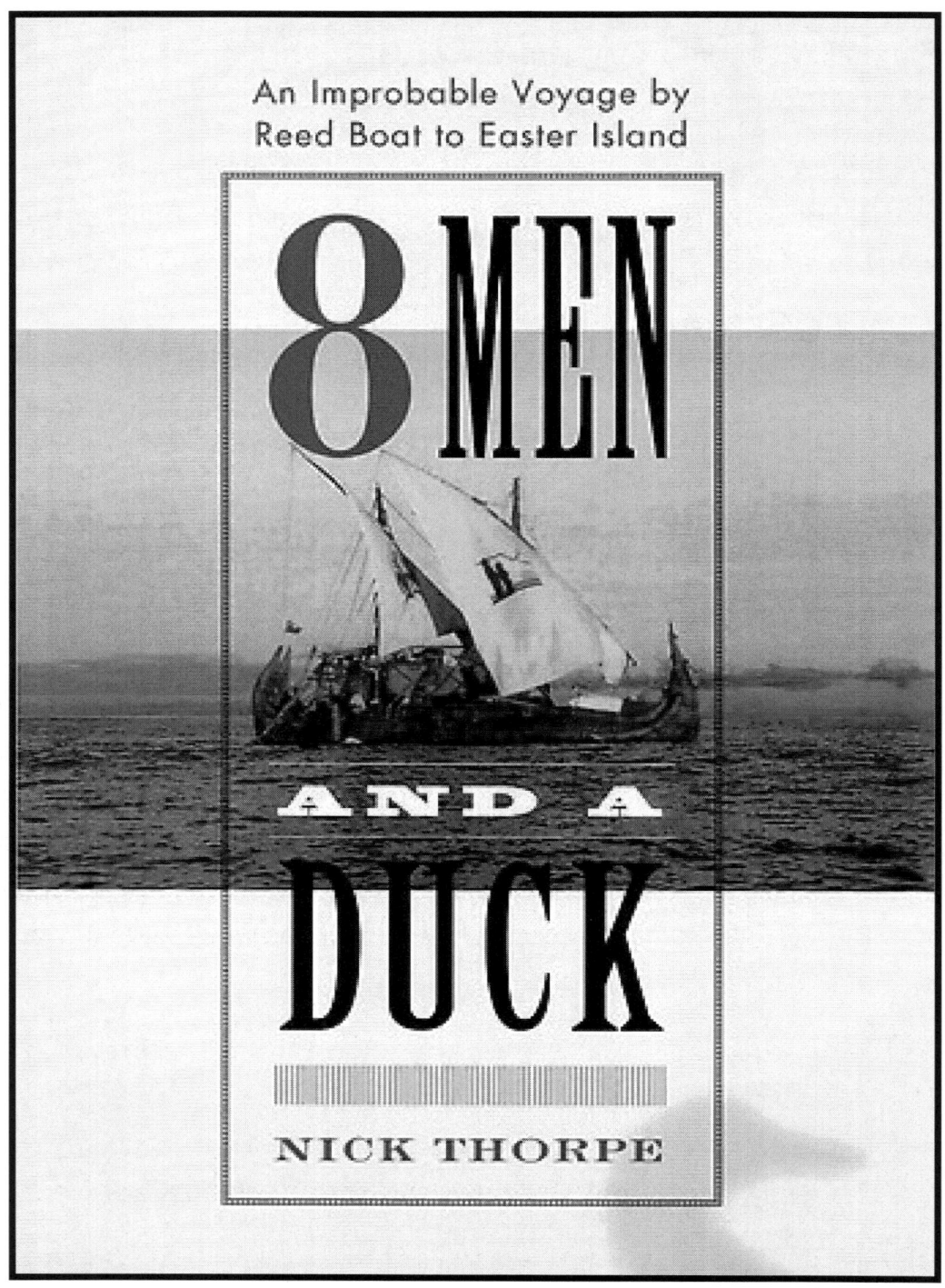

An Improbable Voyage by
Reed Boat to Easter Island

8 MEN
AND A
DUCK

NICK THORPE

Chronicle of the journey by Nick Thorpe

For perhaps the first time ever, or possibly the first time in over a thousand years, depending on your view of the evidence, a reed boat sailed through the gap separating the ancient ceremonial center of Orongo, and the small offshore island of Moto Nui. It was across this gap that the famous annual birdman competition was held, where young men on small reed floats swam and climbed to reach the first sooty tern egg of each spring.

At 3:00 in the afternoon of Sunday, April 9th, 2000, Viracocha I anchored at Hanga Piko, where the arrival of a reed boat from Chile was greeted with decidedly mixed feelings. The memory of nineteenth century raids by Peruvian slavers is still warm on this Polynesian island, and any reminders of ancient ties with the mainland stir complex emotions. Buck himself wanted to preserve Viracocha I, which had survived the voyage in almost perfect condition. Local merchants likewise saw an interesting tourist attraction. But when others recalled the biting mosquitos they felt had arrived with the reeds of Kitin Muñoz' Mata Rangi I, Buck had no choice but to agree to burn the ship. Less than two weeks later, stripped of all useable equipment, Viracocha I went up in flames at Hanga Roa.

Native navigation in Peru and adjoining sections of north-western South America is a subject that is little known and still less understood by modern boat builders, archaeologists and anthropologists. The apparent reason is that Peruvian Native boat building was based on principles entirely different from those of a western mindset. To the European brain the only seaworthy vessel is one made buoyant by a watertight, air-filled hull, so big and high that it cannot be filled by the waves. But to the ancient Peruvians the only seaworthy craft was one which could never be filled by water because its open construction formed no receptacle to retain the invading seas, which washed through. They achieved this by building exceedingly buoyant rafts of Balsa wood.

This type of Peruvian Balsa raft could travel as far as the islands of Polynesia, 4000 miles away, as Heyerdahl proved with Kon Tiki. The first record of a Peruvian Balsa raft antedates the actual discovery of the Inca Empire. When Francisco Pizarro left the Panama Isthmus in 1526 on his second voyage of discovery down the Pacific coast of South America; his expedition found Peruvian merchants sailors at sea long before he discovered their country.

Early Spanish drawing of a Peruvian sailing craft

His Pilot was sailing ahead to explore the coast southwards near the equator, when off northern Ecuador his ship suddenly met another sailing vessel of almost equal size, coming in the opposite direction.

The raft was manned by 20 Indian men and women, 11 of whom were thrown overboard, four were left with the raft, and two men and three women were retained by the Spanish to be trained as interpreters for later voyages. The Spaniards estimated the raft capacity at 36 tons, only a fraction less than their own vessel.

Their report stated that it carried masts and yards of very fine wood, and cotton sails in the same shape and manner as on their own ships. It had very good rigging of hemp, stronger than their own rope, and mooring stones for anchors. Many similar accounts described rafts made of long and light logs, always of odd number, 5,7,9 or 11, tied together with cross beams and covered by a deck. The larger ones had the ability to carry up to 50 men and three horses, and had a special cooking place on board in a thatched hut. The cargoes often included salt, another proof of their seaworthiness. (14)

A maritime exchange system, prior to European "contact" stretched from the west coast of Mexico to southernmost Peru, trading mostly in spondylus, which represented rain, fertility and was considered the principal food of the gods by the people of the Inca confederation (erroneously, in my view, called an "empire.") Spondylus was used in elite rituals and the effective redistribution of it had political effect in the Andes during the pre-Hispanic times. (15) It was in fact the rafts of the Chincha culture, located to the south of modern day Lima and including the Paracas Peninsula, who were the great navigators and sailors prior to the arrival of the Inca in the area in the 15th century. And, in fact, spondylus jewelry found in graves of the Paracas culture, dating from 800 BC to 200 AD, hint that the Paracas themselves were capable of visiting and trading with the natives of the coast of Ecuador during this period.

Royal Paracas person with Spondylus shell adornments

What this all indicates is that not only were pre-Colombian sea farers in existence on the coast of Peru, but had the capability to make long distance voyaging, and could have reached Rapa Nui as the Viracocha I showed was possible.

And then of course there are the plants that exist on both Rapa Nui and the western areas of Peru. The most obvious and lauded is the sweet potato, or Kumara, (camote being the common Peruvian name) which Heyerdahl and others have used, effectively to show that human contact between the two areas in the distant past is probable, as the kumara would unlikely be carried by birds, or float on its own across the great expanse of the ocean.

The center of origin and domestication of sweet potato is thought to be either in Central America or South America, and most likely the former, where they were domesticated at least 5,000 years ago. (16) The plant, most likely in the form of cuttings, had most likely been spread by local people to the Caribbean and South America by 2500 BC, with Peru most likely being one of the last places on the continent where it proliferated, due to its geographic distance from the Central American source.

The humble yet vitally important sweet potato

The sweet potato was also grown before western exploration in Polynesia. It has been radiocarbon-dated in the Cook Islands to 1000 AD, and current thinking is that it was brought to central Polynesia around 700 AD, possibly by Polynesians who had traveled to South America and back, and spread across Polynesia to Hawaii and New Zealand from there. (17) However, as we have just seen, it is also very likely that people, aka the Long Ears from the coast of South America could have brought the sweet potato with them when they visited and possibly settled Rapa Nui.

Other plants of interest include the totora reed, most famously native to Lake Titicaca in Peru and Bolivia, where it has been used in the making of boats, houses and even floating islands by the Uru people for thousands of years. (18) It is also prevalent along the mid coast of Peru, where the native people have used totora to build their caballitos de totora, small rowed and straddled fishing vessels, for at least 3,000 years. Surprisingly to most, The Rapa Nui people of Easter Island used totora reeds - locally known as *nga'atu*, for thatching and to make *Pora* (swimming aids). These are used for recreation, and were formerly employed by *hopu* (clan champions) to reach offshore Motu Nui in the *Tangata manu* (bird-man) competition. How the plant arrived on the island is not clear; Thor Heyerdahl argued that it had been brought by prehistoric Peruvians but it is also likely to have been brought by birds. In any case, recent work indicates that totora has been growing on Easter Island for at least 30,000 years. (19)

Totora reed double hull craft still in use on Lake Titicaca

However, what has seemingly not been addressed is that the name they call their craft made from this material is practically the same, save one letter, on both Rapa Nui and in Peru; Pora in the former, and Tora in the latter. Even if birds had carried the seeds thousands of years before humans supposedly set foot on ships to cross the Pacific, it is clearly likely that they, the visitors and/or settlers would have brought such a useful plant on their voyages. Had their ships been made of totora, some would also have been brought for purposes of hull repair, etc., though not necessarily in "living" form.

Manioc, gourd, and another plant known to the Rapa Nui islanders as *tavari*, used as a medicinal plant, are all originally from South America, but also grow on Rapa Nui. Like the totora, tavari grows in Lake Titicaca. This last information supports the case for contact with Tiahuanaco (Tiwanaku.) Manioc is also called cassava, and more specifically yucca in Peru, where it is still a commonly eaten starchy tuber.

5/ When Was The Island First Settled?

Orthodox researchers believe that Easter Island was settled only once: by Polynesians in the 4th century AD, or perhaps even as late as the 10th, depending on the source. Since no seafarers in those days are supposed to have had maps, it is thought that the island must have been discovered mainly by chance, and that such an unlikely event could not possibly have happened more than once. As John Flenley and Paul Bahn put it: *'The chances of Easter Island being reached even once were extremely limited; to imagine it being reached several times over vast distances is beyond belief.'* (20) Some of the island's legends, however, imply two or three different migrations. As is often the case, native traditions, depending on the source are sometimes contradictory and cannot all be historically accurate, but they offer important clues. My trip to Rapa Nui, with my wife in February 2012 allowed me to ask some of the descendants of the people their story as to the story of their origins. This is of course a very complex issue, but as a hint they told me that rather than being the last, or one of the last places to be discovered and settled in "Polynesia" it was in fact the first.

Maori people of Aotearoa, especially those of the Waitaha, state very firmly that their ancestors came from Rapa Nui, and not from Tahiti, which most western scholars firmly believe. If this is the case, then perhaps it adds to our theory that these first ancestors of Rapa Nui were not Polynesian at all, but came from elsewhere. As the wind and sea current patterns tend to make the coast of present day Peru the most direct and likely candidate, this adds fuel to the idea that the Paracas or other cultures we previously discussed could have been the source of migration to Rapa Nui early on.

I was not allowed to quote my Rapa Nui sources directly, as they insisted their identities be protected, mainly due to the fact that I may inadvertently misquote them, but they were very firm in their statement; Rapa Nui was populated prior to Aotearoa, Tahiti, the Marquesas, Tuamotus or Hawaii. And as to their ancient sea faring skills, the positioning of many of the Ahu and Moai figures have direct alignments with both solstice and equinox positions, and these were not solely or simply for agricultural timing purposes. And other star related positioning of these stone structures, though I was not able to get detailed information from my sources, are self evident, even today. Star navigation, known as "wayfinding" amongst the Maohi of the Pacific was the secret to their ability to travel, freely and with confidence throughout "Polynesia" and possibly beyond.

In fact, what do the present day living people of Rapa Nui say about how difficult it could have been, or in fact today is, to navigate to the island from of Tahiti, from which later waves of migrants obviously came? According to a member of a Rapa Nui royal family I met in Hawaii in 1996, whose name I shall not reveal her actual identity for privacy reasons, the sea path from Tahiti to Rapa Nui was used for centuries, the last navigator sailor being one of her relatives, in the 1950s. He not only traveled to Rapa Nui from Tahiti, but completed the return voyage, perhaps more than once.

My source also stated that she was a major informant when a modern day traditional sailing craft wished to follow the ancient sea routes from Tahiti to Rapa Nui, and her knowledge was based on both oral traditions passed down in her family, and what her father, the 1950's sailor and navigator had told her.

Lapita is a term applied to an ancient Pacific Ocean archaeological culture which is believed by many archaeologists to be the common ancestor of several cultures in Polynesia, Micronesia, and some coastal areas of Melanesia. The archaeological culture and its characteristic geometric dentate stamped pottery are named after the type of site where it was first uncovered in the Foué peninsula on Grand Terre, the main island of New Caledonia. The excavation was carried out in 1952 by American archaeologists Edward W. Gifford and Richard Shulter Jr at 'Site 13'. (21)

Examples of Lapita pottery designs

The settlement and pottery shards were later dated to 800 BC and proved significant in research on the early peopling of the Pacific Islands. More than two hundred Lapita sites have since been uncovered, ranging more than 4000km from coastal and island Melanesia to Fiji and Tonga with its most eastern limit so far in Samoa. In Western Polynesia, Lapita pottery is found from 800 BC onwards in the Fiji-Samoa-Tonga area. From Tonga and Samoa, Polynesian culture spread to Eastern Polynesia areas including the Marquesas and the Society Islands, and then later to Hawaii, Easter Island, and New Zealand. However, pottery making did not persist in most of Polynesia, mainly due to the lack of suitable clay on small islands.

Many scientists believe Lapita pottery in Melanesia to be proof that Polynesians passed through this area on their way into the central Pacific, despite only circumstantial evidence connecting Lapita with Polynesia. Plain ware pottery, as in without ornamentation is found on many Polynesian islands and was thought to be a significant player in the transformation of Lapita society into a Polynesian cultural complex. Unfortunately no classical Polynesian artefacts have been found within this plain ware assemblage. Archaeological evidence indicates that plain ware pottery ceases abruptly in Samoa around 0BC, being replaced by classic Polynesian cultural complex. This clearly indicates a change in the control of the islands, from the waning Lapita settlers to a culture that used gourds, two-piece fishhooks, trolling lures, harpoon heads, tanged adzes, stone pounders and tattooing needles; none of which are found amongst Lapita artifacts. (22)

According to archaeologist Anita Smith: "Although ceramics have been used as the primary material culture correlate for cultural change in West Polynesia, they are perhaps least suited to identifying Ancestral Polynesians in the archaeological record. Ceramics were not manufactured by Polynesian societies at any time in East Polynesian prehistory. Therefore trying to connect Lapita and plain ware pottery with Polynesians is illogical." (23)

Other attempts to link Lapita culture with Polynesians are similarity in, for example, the techniques used to shape, grind and sand adzes and other stone tools. So, very little direct evidence indeed, and much speculation. Unfortunately, as often occurs, if academics "say it is so" then the general public accepts it, blindly. But what do the oral traditions of the people say?

The various Polynesian cultures each have distinct but related oral traditions that is, legends or myths traditionally considered to recount the history of ancient times (the time of "Po") and the adventures of gods ("Atua") and deified ancestors. The accounts are characterised by extensive use of allegory, metaphor, parable, hyperbole, and personification.

The Maori of New Zealand (Aotearoa) especially, as well as some Hawaiians believe that the homeland of all of the Polynesian people, more correctly known as the Maori (Aotearoa, Tahiti and Rapanui) and Maoli (Hawaii) is a real land called Hawaiki. Of course, the similarity to the name Hawaii is obvious, but most believe that it represents the island, in Tahiti more commonly known as Raiatea.

When European scholars began to investigate tribal traditions in depth, some were taken by stories concerning Hawaiki. Given the ubiquity of Hawaiki in tribal traditions – all describe Hawaiki as some kind of originating point – some Europeans attempted to understand more.

One scholar was S. Percy Smith, the founding president of the Polynesian Society and author of numerous texts on tribal history and traditions. In his book *Hawaiki, the original homeland of the Maori* (1904), Smith advanced his theories as to the physical location of Hawaiki. He suggested that islands such as Savaiʻi in Samoa, Hawaii and even Java near Indonesia were actually Hawaiki in localised forms. His method was to develop a view on the origins of the Māori people by analysing the traditions held by Māori in his time. This method had widespread acceptance and many scholars, both Māori and European, were excited by his conclusions. (24)

Criticisms of Smith's methodology are numerous, but two presented by Margaret Orbell in *Hawaiki: a new approach to Maori tradition* (1985) are particularly telling. First, she suggests that it is inappropriate to view tribal traditions as historical; in other words, they should not be read literally as a record of actual events. She argues that by the time Europeans arrived in New Zealand, iwi (native) traditions were on the whole mythical in character. In her view the 'memory' of a Polynesian homeland was transformed into myth over a long period. Therefore, it is more useful to interpret iwi traditions as symbolic of past events rather than as a literal representation. Second, she points out that Smith and others were too willing to explain away inconsistencies and to smooth over difficulties. Orbell writes: 'unfortunately they approached their material in such a wildly speculative and uncritical manner that the whole subject ... is now in some disrepute.' (25)

The idea that Raiatea is the homeland of the Maori and Maoli people is given credibility by the presence of Taputapuatea, which is and has been the central marae, or holy place of these people for centuries...at least.

As it is said, by European descended scholars and Native people alike, Tahiti sits at the center of what is known as the Polynesian Triangle; the three points that make up this triangle are Hawaii in the north, Aotearoa to the southwest and Rapa Nui in the southeast. Raiatea, and more specifically Taputapuatea, whose age is unknown, even to the inhabitants of the island, and whose name roughly translates as "the very sacred white place" which does not refer to skin colour, but to purity, was and is the central spiritual place for "the triangle."

Part of the great Marae of Taputapuatea on Raiatea

Raiatea is also known as the homeland of the Gods, namely Tane, Rongo, Tu and Tangaroa, shared by all of the so called Polynesian people, and these Gods, whose home is the summit of the mountain named Temehani, are believed by some to still live there. Interestingly, though these same gods were and are worshipped in Hawaii and other Polynesian Island groups, they were not on Rapa Nui.

Unfortunately, after exhaustive years of research into where the Polynesians came from prior to this, based on oral traditions, I have hit a wall; there is apparently no information, or at least none that I have been able to access, through books, the internet, and even my journey there some time ago. So how did the people of Rapa Nui arrive on their island, and when according to their own traditions?

According to legend, a powerful supernatural being named Uoke, who came from a land called Hiva, travelled about the Pacific prying up whole islands with a gigantic lever and tossing them into the sea where they vanished beneath the waves. After destroying many islands he came to the coast of Easter Island, then a much larger land than it is today, and began to lever up parts of it and cast them into the sea. Eventually he reached a place on the island where the rocks were so sturdy that his lever broke. He was unable to dispose of the last fragment, and this remained as the island we know today.

Easter Island's culture was founded by the legendary god-king Hotu Matua ("prolific father"), who is said to have lived on a remnant of Hiva called Maori, in a locality called Marae Renga. According to one version of the legend, he set sail for Easter Island due to the cataclysm caused by Uoke. Another version says he was forced to flee after being defeated in war. After a magician in Hiva called Hau Maka had made an astral journey to Easter Island in a dream, a reconnaissance voyage of seven youths was sent there, and Hotu Matu'a followed later in a double-canoe. (26)

Ahu Akivi: The 7 Moai are said to represent 7 navigators sent to find land by Hotu Matu'a

The most widespread tradition today is that Hotu Matua's homeland was a large, warm, green island to the *west* of Easter Island, but a tradition told to the earliest European explorers says that the first settlers came from a land to the east, known as Marae-toe-hau, 'the burial place', which had a very hot climate. (27) This very much describes the dry desert climate of Peru. One tradition suggests that the first Polynesian migration, led by Hotu Matua, was followed by a second Polynesian migration about 100 years later. References are also made to several voyages being made back and forth to Hiva.

Many of the Marquesas Islands, such as Nuku Hiva have "Hiva" in their name

There are indications that Easter Island was inhabited even before Hotu Matu'a arrived. According to one tradition, when Hau Maka had his prophetic dream, he saw six men on the island. Another mentions that Hoto Matua's seven explorers found an inhabitant on the island, who had arrived with another person who had since died. (28)

A third account says that a burial platform was found at Hotu Matua's landing place, and a network of stone-paved roads built by earlier settlers was found inland. (29) This may prove key to the idea that there were in fact two distinct periods of construction on Rapa Nui, very refined stone walls, small in size and referred to as temple bases, or Ahu, as well as the first of the great head, and or head/body figures called Moai. But this we shall get into later.

Large skulls such as these from Easter Island are presently unaccounted for

Francis Mazière, who conducted archaeological excavations on the island in 1963, was told by a native elder that 'very big men, but not giants, lived on the island well before the coming of Hotu Matua'. Another related the following legend:

"The first men to live on the island were the survivors of the world's first race. They were yellow, very big, with long arms, great stout chests, huge ears although their lobes were not stretched: they had pure yellow hair and their bodies were hairless and shining. They did not possess fire. This race once existed on two other Polynesian islands. They came by boat from a land that lies behind America." (30)

The key players in the island's traditional history are the Hanau e'epe and the Hanau momoko. These terms are often translated Long Ears and Short Ears respectively. However, some researchers say that this is erroneous, and that the correct translations are 'stocky race' and 'slender race'. Hanau means 'race' or 'ethnic group'. *E'epe* means 'stocky' or 'corpulent', but there is also a word epe, which means 'earlobe'. Thor Heyerdahl says that the term was formerly spelled Hanau epe. Whatever the correct term may be, the people referred to certainly had elongated earlobes. Today momoko carries the sense of 'sharp-pointed', and it is assumed that the word probably used to mean 'slender' or 'weak'. Some writers have concluded that the Hanau e'epe were the upper class, and the Hanau momoko the lower class. (31)

The Long Ears reportedly subjugated the Short Ears, until the latter finally rebelled. All the long-ears except one were allegedly massacred in the latter half of the 17th century; after a fierce battle the short-ears drove them into the Poike ditch, in which piles of brushwood had been set alight. Most researchers doubt this story, as no weapons or bones have ever been found in the ditch. Although some charcoal excavated from it has been radiocarbon dated to about 1676, other charcoal has been dated to about 386 AD and to the 11th century, and it could all have come from bush fires or slash-and-burn practices used in clearing the fields. In any event, it is unlikely that only one Long Ear survived such a battle, since a period of civil war followed when all the long-eared statues were overthrown, and there were still people with elongated earlobes alive when the first Europeans arrived.

In contrast with the powerfully supernatural origin myths of many of the world's indigenous cultures, the story of Hotu Matu'a is actually probable in many respects. Glottochronology, a linguistic analysis technique that aims to determine when languages with common root tongues separated from each other, indicates that the language of Rapa Nui contains many Polynesian place names and a strong structural commonality with an archaic central eastern Polynesian dialect, as well as elements of an archaic western Polynesian dialect that would have only been present in earlier forms of the central eastern tongue. Using these criteria, it has been surmised that the people of Rapa Nui split completely apart from the rest of Polynesia sometime between 300 and 550 AD, probably voyaging from the westerly Marquesas, or (more likely) the central eastern Mangareva or Pitcairn. The linguistic evidence corresponds with a recent count of 57 generations since Hotu Matu'a which, judging by an average of 25 years per generation, would place an approximate date of 450 AD for the founding population. The earliest firm radiocarbon dates for human habitation on the island are from Ahu Tahai on the island's southwest corner (near Hanga Roa), and date to 690 AD plus or minus 130 years; this data is also consistent with legend since it would have taken sometime before the first Ahu's construction. Questions as to the historical trajectory of the island have been contentious for decades. Many theories have been propounded about comings and goings to the island from South America as well as later migrations from Polynesia. More recently, the archaeologists Terry Hunt and Carl Lipo have pursued the hypothesis that the island was not colonized until the 12th-13th centuries AD; however, current paleo-environmental and linguistic evidence points to a single migration and an earlier settlement which is consistent with legend. (32)

Rapa Nui's southwest corner seems to have been colonized first, and it is here where introduced Polynesian species of plants and animals would have initially been nurtured in this new environment. Due to the climate being slightly colder, drier, and windier than most of Polynesia, however, certain staple domesticates (such as the breadfruit and coconut) did not grow. In addition, there is no evidence of the presence of dogs and pigs on the island before European contact. At the north coast's Anakena, the legendary landing site of Hotu Matu'a, the first habitations seem to date to the 8th or 9th centuries AD, with the first Ahu built here by 1100 CE. The south coast didn't build up until around 1300 AD, when monumental construction on the island peaked; the Ahu and Moai.

View of Ahu Tahai

6/ The Ahu and Moai

Rapa Nui has at least 313 ceremonial platforms or ahu; open-air temple sanctuaries erected in honour of the gods and deified ancestors. A few were built inland but most are situated around the coast, usually at sheltered coves and areas favourable for human habitation, though a few are located on cliff edges. They are composed of a rubble core faced with masonry, for which no mortar was used. Seaward walls often consist of uncut stones, but sometimes they consist of precisely carved and fitted blocks. On the landward side was a ramp, paved with lines of beach boulders and sloping down to an artificially levelled plaza.

Lone Moai at Ahu Ko te Triku, part of the Ahu Tahai complex

Some Ahu are quite small, but others are remarkable pieces of massive communal engineering, 150 m (500 ft) or more long and up to 7 m (23 ft) high. Some required the moving of 300 to 500 tons of stone, while the Ahu Tahai complex comprised three structures requiring 23,000 cubic metres of rock and earth fill, weighing an estimated 2000 tons.

Platforms served as social and religious centres, and also as boundary markers. A few platforms seem to have been built to contain burials, but this does not seem to have been the original function of the image platforms. No early skeletons have been discovered, whereas elaborate cremation pits have been found behind the central platform at many complexes, in contrast to the rest of central and eastern Polynesia, where cremation was not practised. At a later stage, bodies were interred in stone-lined tombs in the platforms and ramps. After the Moai had been toppled, bodies were placed around the fallen Moai or on other parts of ramps and then covered with stones. Semi-pyramidal platforms were the last type of Ahu to be built: they were usually superimposed on the earlier, statue-bearing platforms, and seem to have been designed purely for burial purposes. Less than 75 are known, compared with more than 125 image platforms. (32a)

Almost full view of Ahu Tongariki

The official position is that all Easter Island's platforms are simply variations of the Marae platforms of central and eastern Polynesia, which were socio-religious centres and shrines to ancestral gods. Vinapu's megalithic stone wall is said to bear only a superficial resemblance to the classic 'Incan' masonry because, unlike the solid block construction used in Peru, the Easter Island walls are merely a facing of slabs that mask a rubble core.

Detail of the front wall at Ahu Vinapu

However, there are also striking similarities with the pre-Incan Andean style of masonry. Each slab is convex or pillow-shaped, with slightly bevelled edges, and stones with projecting edges are fitted into stones with receding edges. The blocks are irregularly shaped, fit together with the utmost precision, and small holes or chinks are filled with perfectly fitted stones. A block in one corner of the Ahu Vinapu wall has a projecting knob, just like many large blocks in Peru. The corners of the seawall are rounded, and its entire face is in fact slightly convex, again as in the Andes. Prof. Camila Laureani, a connoisseur of Tiwanaku and 'Inca' type masonry writes: 'Ahu Vinapu is an architectonic construction which combines the essential characteristics of the structures in the Altiplano of Peru-Bolivia in a manner so evident that one cannot doubt the arrival on the island of a contingent of these people.' (32b)

Wall detail at the Coricancha in Cusco Peru

Around 20 Ahu appear to have been oriented astronomically, so that the Moai faced the rising or setting sun at the solstices or equinoxes. The inland Ahu with astronomical orientation are generally linked with the solstices, especially the winter solstice, though the Moai of Ahu Akivi face the setting sun at the equinoxes. Astronomically oriented ahu along the coast tend to be positioned so that the Moai look straight east or west.

Graham Hancock, author of such books as "Fingerprints Of The Gods" points out that Ra, the name of the Egyptian sun god, appears frequently in connection with Easter Island's sacred architecture, its mythical past, and its cosmology. Raa means 'sun' in the island's language. There were clans called Raa, Hitti-ra (sunrise), and Ura-o-Hehe (red setting sun), the crater lakes are named Rano Kao, Rano Aroi, and Rano Raraku, and Ahu Ra'ai was aligned to two volcanic peaks to act as a marker and observatory for the path of the sun on the December solstice. (32c)

Sunset at Ahu Tahai

Traditions state that ages ago there existed on the island a brotherhood of 'learned men who studied the sky', the Tangata Rani. Katherine Routledge was taken to a northwest facing cave near Ahu Tahi and told it had been 'a place where priests taught constellations and the ways of the stars to apprentices'. Near the eastern extremity of the Poike headland she was shown a large flat rock called papa Ui Hetu'u, or 'rock where they watched the stars', incised with a spiral design. Nearby there is another engraved stone on which 10 cup-shaped depressions are visible, which are said to have represented a star map.

While Rapa Nui's monumental architecture developed into highly distinct forms, analogous examples can be found in traditional Polynesia. The Ahu platforms have clear antecedents in the *Marae* platforms of Tahiti, where wooden Moai-like figures and smaller stone idols were erected. On Rapa Nui, Moai represent respected ancestors and chiefs, often serving as funerary monuments. With their great size and stately form, they likely served as a type of sacred border between the terrestrial world and the heavens; between life and death. Positioned on Ahu, the Moai of the coast faced inland; they were said to be infused with the Mana (spiritual power) of the persons they were dedicated to. These Moai exercised considerable power over the island, a power which likely included a solid territorial stake for the descendants of the persons they represented. As social boundaries seem to have been fairly strong between the different chiefdoms, and likely got more defined through the early 11th-16th centuries AD, it has been inferred that the bulk of the Moai carving and Ahu construction was undertaken not by a centralized authority but by individual chiefdoms. (33)

As is stated above, the conventional belief by academics is that most, if not all Moai, and the Ahu altars of Rapanui were made between the 11th and 16th centuries AD. Most of the Moai were made of volcanic tuff, which is a relatively soft material. However, 53 of the known 887 are of harder stone, in some cases basalt. In fact, there are 13 Moai carved from basalt, 22 from trachyte and 17 from fragile red scoria. (34)

One of the few Moai whose eyes have been remade

Polynesian Tiki on the Marquesas Islands

A basic description of the Moai is as follows. They are monolithic statues, their minimalist style related to forms found throughout Polynesia. Moai are carved in relatively flat planes, the faces bearing proud but enigmatic expressions. The over-large heads (a three-to-five ratio between the head and the body, a sculptural trait that demonstrates the Polynesian belief in the sanctity of the chiefly head) have heavy brows and elongated noses with a distinctive fish-hook-shaped curl of the nostrils. The lips protrude in a thin pout. Like the nose, the ears are elongated and oblong in form. The jaw lines stand out against the truncated neck. The torsos are heavy, and, sometimes, the clavicles are subtly outlined in stone. The arms are carved in bas relief and rest against the body in various positions, hands and long slender fingers resting along the crests of the hips, meeting at the Hami (loincloth), with the thumbs sometimes pointing towards the navel. Generally, the anatomical features of the backs are not detailed, but sometimes bear a ring and girdle motif on the buttocks and lower back. The navel focus could very well indicate that their home land and perhaps that of other people, including those found in other parts of "Polynesia" was Rapa Nui. Or, could represent the "sunken" land referred to as Hiva.

Reproductions of Moai showing detail

What has perhaps attracted the most attention about the Moai is that many don't appear, in general, to "look Polynesian." The noses especially, being oblong on some, are in contrast to what may be described as the more common flattened ones of Polynesians. Was this an artistic expression, or an indication that the Moai were not meant to portray Hotu Matu'a and his descendants? The informants I have on Rapa Nui vehemently insist that they are the direct likenesses of specific ancestors for whom the sculptures/grave figures were constructed.

Dr. Robert Schoch, the American geologist from Boston University, who was a pivotal force in proving that the Sphinx in Egypt is clearly far older than the "accepted" date by Egyptologists of around 2500 BC. In his own words:

Dr. Robert Schoch and wife Katie at Ahu Vinapu November 2012

'In 1990 I first traveled to Egypt, with the sole purpose of examining the Great Sphinx from a geological perspective. I assumed that the Egyptologists were correct in their dating, but soon I discovered that the geological evidence was not compatible with what the Egyptologists were saying. On the body of the Sphinx, and on the walls of the Sphinx Enclosure (the pit or hollow remaining after the Sphinx's body was carved from the bedrock), I found heavy erosional features (seen in the accompanying photographs) that I concluded could only have been caused by rainfall and water runoff. The thing is, the Sphinx sits on the edge of the Sahara Desert and the region has been quite arid for the last 5000 years. Furthermore, various structures securely dated to the Old Kingdom show only erosion that was caused by wind and sand (very distinct from the water erosion). To make a long story short, I came to the conclusion that the oldest portions of the Great Sphinx, what I refer to as the core-body, must date back to an earlier period (at least 5000 B.C., and maybe as early as 7000 or 9000 B.C.), a time when the climate was very different and included more rain.' (35)

One of the exposed Moai inside the Rano Raraku crater

When he visited Rapa Nui, albeit briefly in January of 2010, Schoch was particularly impressed by the varying degrees of weathering and erosion seen on different Moai, which could be telltale signs of major discrepancies in their ages. The levels of sedimentation around certain Moai also impressed him. Some Moai have been buried in up to an estimated six meters (20 feet) of sediment, or more, such that even though they are standing erect, only their chins and heads are above the current ground level. Such high levels of sedimentation could occur quickly, for instance, if there were catastrophic landslides or mudflows, but Schoch could not find any such evidence (and landslides would tend to shift and knock over the tall statues). Rather, to his eye, the sedimentation around certain Moai suggests a much more extreme antiquity than most conventional archaeologists and historians believe to be the case.

Not only does sedimentation around the statues suggest a longer and different chronology than conventionally accepted, but so too do weathering and erosion patterns, and stylistic considerations. Although on one level most of the Moai are stylistically similar and even stereotypic, at another level each is unique and they could, Schoch believes, be categorized according to stylistic considerations.

What many people do not realize is that all of the Moai are complete representations of humans, as in heads, necks and full torsos with arms. The only examples which are solely heads, or heads with necks are those which are broken.

Broken Moai at Rano Raraku quarry; head to the right, face down

Excavation of a Moai inside Rano Raraku crater

One of the excavated Moai showing that they have full bodies

The Moai should, in addition, according to Schoch be sorted according to lithology (stone type) as well as weathering and erosion levels (taking orientation and relative exposure to the elements into account). Another key to solving the problem will be to compare weathering, erosion, and sedimentation rates in historical times. Schoch has begun to gather photographs of various Moai and landforms on Easter Island taken over the last 130 years so as to compare them geologically to their conditions today, and in this way attempt to get a quantitative handle on weathering, erosion, and sedimentation rates.

Moai head seemingly recycled into the Ahu at Anakena

The earliest Moai appear to have been more finely worked from harder stone such as basalt, compared to the volcanic tuffs of most Moai, which appear to date from later periods. The few surviving basalt Moai have been found at deeper stratigraphic levels below other Moai and the platforms upon which they were erected, or were reused in later structures—thus indicating the basalt Moai are among the earliest on the island. Furthermore, at least one of the basalt Moai (now housed in the museum on Easter Island) is of a very strange form; with an elongated head and well-defined breasts it is often considered a female while virtually all other Moai appear to be males.

Another major puzzle, which is directly applicable to the chronology and dating of the Moai, is the matter of where they were quarried. Quarries on the rim of the volcanic crater, where large Moai were carved from the volcanic tuffs, are well exposed and still contain partially carved sculptures still in place.

One of the Moai still in the quarry of Rano Raraku

Based on the geology of Easter Island, Schoch expects that any suitable basalt deposits, from which the harder stone Moai came from, would occur lower in the stratigraphic section, so low in fact that they might currently be under sea level off the coast of the island. Sea levels have risen dramatically since the end of the last ice age, on average 350 feet globally, some ten thousand or more years ago, and if the basalt Moai were quarried along the coast of Easter Island from areas since inundated by the sea, this could help to date them, and is immediately suggestive that they are thousands of years older than conventionally believed to be the case. Also, while the later standard Moai carved of volcanic tuffs could be relatively easily cut out of the rock using primitive tools found in abundance on the island, the same cannot be said for the apparently earlier and more sophisticated basalt Moai, which may have formed the model and set the standard for the later volcanic tuff ones. (36)

A volcanic tuff Moai still in the quarry awaiting its release

Unusual basalt Moai in the local museum, presumed to be female

Such a concept, based on a clearly reliable geologist like Robert Schoch, fits in well with the idea that Rapa Nui was populated, for an extensive period of time, by two separate peoples; one, who were masters of hard stone sculpture and wall (Ahu) building, and another, that was most likely put into service, whether voluntarily or by force, to replicate the earlier works.

Another exposed Moai

In November of 2012 I traveled to Rapa Nui with Robert Schoch, his wife, my wife, and Hugh Newman of the group Megalithomania, along with 20 guests, and it was especially Dr. Schoch's geological knowledge and insights which I wanted learn about and present here.

The reason why the Moai of the Rano Raraku quarry area were buried, according to my Rapa Nui informants was that a specific event happened, sometime in the 16th or 17th centuries AD.

Once a Moai had been quite finely shaped on the top and side, and was released from the bedrock underneath, it "walked" down the Rano Raraku hill and was placed into a pit in order that final finishing work, especially to the back, could be conducted. The quarry area was of course a major work site on the island, perhaps THE major undertaking over the course of several centuries or more, and oral tradition states that on one specific day it shut down, never to be worked at again.

The story centers on a woman who was the spiritual mother figure of sorts, overseer of all that occurred at Rano Raraku. When she was denied food one day by fishermen who had caught an enormous lobster, destined for the workers on the Moai, she evoked a spell which caused all work to stop. Of course, even if this is a true story, the simplicity of the tale is not the full story. What it intimates is that the culture of Rapa Nui by this time had undergone some form of erosion; people no longer assisted each other in mutually beneficial, and perhaps especially the ritual tasks that held them together. The stoppage of the making of Moai, supposedly in one fell swoop although that has never been proven, almost immediately seems to have coincided with loss of faith in the Hanau eèpe, and their demise.

It is also at this time that the Bird Man cult, Tangata Manu is believed to have begun, replacing a hierarchical system of social order, Long Ears and Short Ears with one based on a yearly competition; the retrieval, by the first returning althete, of a sooty tern bird egg from the nesting grounds on Motu Nui, a nearby island.

With the Moai sitting in their "finishing pits" over the course of up to 500 years, to present, natural soil erosion would have at least partially filled the pits, and the shame of the makers' descendants, a sense instilled and fuelled by Catholic missionaries, could very well have finished the job. Though more than 200 of the Moai can presently be observed at Rano Raraku in various states of "burial," some of my local informants told me, on my 2012 visit, that many more are completely below ground, and intact. The debate is clearly were they abandoned and/or buried on purpose after the fall of the Long Ears? Or are they much older than that?

Certain traditions, and speculation by western scholars relate that the Hanau e`epe brought Moai carving and other civilized arts to Easter Island, and that they generally dominated, and even enslaved, the Hanau momoko. This situation ended when the Hanau momoko rebelled against their masters, drove the Hanau e`epe to one corner of the island, and in an epic battle all or almost all (traditions vary) of the Hanau e'epe were killed. Whether the Hanau e'epe arrived first or last we have endeavoured to ascertain in earlier parts of the book.

It is highly unlikely that they came afterwards, because, if the theory is that they were lighter skinned people from the coast of Peru, and in fact the Inca, what is now known from my research, and that of others, such as David Hatcher Childress and others is that the Inca themselves were not great stone masons. They were not responsible for the construction of the best known enigmatic hard stone works such as those found around Cuzco, and in the Sacred Valley of Peru, such as the Coricancha, Sachsayhuaman and Ollantayambo, as well as the Sun Temple and Hitching Post of the Sun at Machu Picchu. These predate the Inca by thousands of years, because they display the clear presence of technological prowess which the Inca did not have.

In the archaeological record, the Inca only possessed bronze chisels and stone hammers, tools which could not have produced the "can't fit a human hair in between the stones" accuracy seen at the above sites. For more information as regards this, I wish to refer you to some of my own books, located at www.brienfoerster.com/books, and www.hiddenincatours.com/buy-ebooks.

7/ Population Decline And Ecocide

Clearly a struggle did ensue between the two races that Roggeveen witnessed when he visited in 1722, but when exactly, and why? He states that they were "of all shades of colour, yellow, white and brown" and did not record any strife occurring between these people, who were clearly from different genetic, and therefore most likely cultural origins. In 1770 a Spanish party from Peru claimed the island for Spain. A conflict seems to have raged on the island before the arrival of the British navigator Captain James Cook four years later. He found a decimated, poverty-stricken population, and observed that the Moai veneration seemed to have ended, as most of the statues had been pulled down. It's possible that some of the statues were toppled even before the Dutch and Spanish visits but that those sailors did not visit the same sites as Cook. (37) Notice that I used the term "some" as compared to "all." It has been the theory, largely or wholly by western academics that the toppling of the Moai occurred prior to European contact, and not later. This we shall delve into later in some depth.

Captain James Cook's crew on Rapa Nui

The Frenchman La Pérouse visited Easter Island in 1786 and found the population calm and prosperous, suggesting a quick recovery from any catastrophe. In 1804 a Russian visitor reported that at least 20 statues were still standing. Accounts from subsequent years suggest another period of destruction so that perhaps only a handful of statues were still standing a decade later. Some of the statues still upright at the beginning of the 19th century were knocked down by western expeditions, and quite possibly as a result, later on of influence from the Catholic Church, who likely regarded these ancestral creations as "idols."

The British ship HMS Blossom arrived in 1825 and reported seeing no standing statues. Easter Island was approached many times during the 19th century, but by then the islanders had become openly hostile to any attempt to land, and very little new information was reported before the 1860s.

The reason for the precipitous decline in the population of the Rapa Nui people after the first visit by an outsider, as in Roggeveen, is obvious; disease. Whether intentionally or by accident, more likely the latter, contact with Europeans, after having been isolated for centuries, would have made the Rapa Nui people vulnerable to diseases carried by the outsiders.

Modern day harvesting on one of Peru's many guano islands

To add insult to injury of the local population, in 1862, Peruvian slave ships took at least 1,000 people (and supposedly most of the male population), to work the Guano Islands of Lima. Included in this group of slaves were the king, his son, and most of the native priests, including those that could read Rongorongo. 100 survivors were later returned, of which 15 reached their homes (carrying smallpox), which almost finished the population of the island. (38) By 1864, the total remaining island population was 111 (originally estimated at being at least 5,000).

Rapa Nui's population was reduced to the point where some of the dead were not even buried. Tuberculosis, introduced by whalers in the mid-19th century, had already killed several islanders when the first Christian missionary, Eugène Eyraud, died from this disease in 1867. About a quarter of the island's population succumbed along with him. In the previous November the French mariner Jean-Baptiste Dutrou-Bornier transported two missionaries, Kaspar Zumbohm and Theodore Escolan, to Easter Island. He visited the island again in March 1867 to recruit labourers for a plantation in Tahiti, but he then amassed huge gambling debts there. He then acquired the yacht *Aora'i*, and arrived again on Easter Island in April 1868, and set up residence at Mataveri, where he began buying up land from the Rapa Nui. In 1869 he seized Koreto, the wife of a Rapa Nui, and married her. He tried to persuade France to make the island a protectorate, and recruited a faction of Rapanui whom he allowed to abandon their Christianity and revert to their previous faith. With rifles, a cannon, and the burning of huts he and his supporters ran the island for several years as self appointed "governor", and making Koreto Queen.

Dutrou-Bornier then bought up the entire island apart from the missionaries' area around Hanga Roa and moved some of the Rapa Nui to Tahiti to work for his backers. In 1871 the missionaries, having fallen out with Dutrou-Bornier, evacuated all but 171 Rapanui to the Gambier Islands. (38b)

The impact on the oral traditions and memory of the survivors, and those that live on Rapa Nui today, is quite obvious. Such a drastic and quite rapid reduction in a population of people, small to start with, would have no doubt killed off many, if not most of the educated members, and with them would have gone much of the knowledge of their history.

Drawing of Queen Koreto and her daughters

Alexander Salmon, Jr., son of an English Jewish merchant and Tahitian Pōmare Dynasty princess, eventually worked to repatriate workers from his inherited copra plantation around 1878. He eventually bought up all lands on Rapa Nui with the exception of the mission, and was its sole employer. He worked to develop tourism on the island, mainly the selling of wood works and other art to passing ships, and was the principal informant for the British and German archaeological expeditions at that time. He sent several pieces of genuine Rongorongo to his niece's husband, the German consul in Valparaíso, Chile. Salmon sold his holdings to the Chilean government in January 2 1888 and signed as a witness to the cession of the island. He returned to Tahiti in December of that year, having effectively ruled the island from 1878 until the secession to Chile, which came in 1888.

Until 1888, Rapa Nui was unclaimed by any foreign country: The island was an unattractive target for acquisition for it lacked rivers and trees, and a safe anchorage. But into this void stepped Chile, which annexed the island under the impression that it had agricultural potential and strategic possibilities as a naval station. Formal annexation brought little change to the island until 1896 when Chile placed the island under the jurisdiction of the Department of Valparaiso. The island was turned into a vast sheep ranch under the direction of a Valparaiso businessman, Enrique Merlet, who confiscated buildings and all animals left to the Rapa Nui by the missionaries who had fled the island in the wake of Dutrou-Bornier's reign of terror. Islanders were forced to build a stone wall around the village of Hangaroa and, except for work; permission was needed to leave the area even to fetch water from the crater. Those who revolted against these perverse rules were exiled to the continent, few returned.

Severed and sightless Moai head; silent witness to so much destruction

Destitute state of some of the islanders

A Scots Chilean company, Williamson Balfour, was the "owner" of the company and in 1903 they created a subsidiary, The Easter Island Exploitation Company. The entire island outside of Hangaroa village was given over to the commercial production of wool and animal by products. These activities made radical changes in the vegetation of the island as well as on the archaeological sites some of which were destroyed to obtain rock for sheep pens and other structures. Successive Chilean governments continued to contract with the Company which controlled every part of island life, from employment to the food supply. Reports in Chilean newspapers described the pitiful plight of the Rapa Nui who often were clad in rags and lacked such essentials as soap. Supply ships came infrequently and irregularly. At one point, desperate islanders petitioned the government to allow them all to immigrate to Tahiti. Reports of the miserable conditions on the island were verified by Bishop Edwards who came to study the problem of leprosy in 1916. Edwards' ensuing 'crusade' brought some changes but, in general, things were the same on the island into the 1950s.

Instead of renewing the sheep company's contract, in 1953 Chile appointed the Navy to oversee the island. This was not a happy time for the islanders who continued to be confined to the village. Navy rule proved to be much harsher than that of the former sheep ranchers, for they had the manpower and means to enforce their rigid rules. From 1944 to 1958 forty one Rapa Nui tried to escape their island 'prison' in open fishing boats. Some made it to the Tuamotus; at least half disappeared at sea.

But at this time, interest in the island's archaeology brought the Norwegian Archaeological Expedition to the island, followed by restoration projects and systematic surveys begun by William Mulloy, one of the members of the Norwegian Expedition. These projects awakened Chilean authorities to the possibility of attracting tourists to the island and also opened new vistas for islanders.

By 1966, many Rapa Nui had been to continental Chile for schooling or for economic reasons and had become aware of what life was like, outside the island. A revolt by the islanders eventually resulted in Easter Island receiving the status of a civil department and a municipal constitution. Once Civil Law arrived on the island, civil servants from Chile came and this influx greatly influenced the Rapa Nui lifestyle and the economic situation. The most significant changes after 1965 resulted from construction of an airfield and subsequent regular air communication with the outside world. For the first time, tourists and scholars were able to reach this isolated island with relative ease. To meet the demand, hotels, restaurants, and gift shops sprung up and islanders found many economic opportunities in relation to tourism. (39)

This is part of, in fact much of, the reason why Rapa Nui is such an obscure place, and why it attracts global attention as a place of mystery. In the latter years of the 20th century and the first years of the 21st century various writers and scientists have advanced theories regarding the rapid decline of Easter Island's magnificent civilization prior to the time of the first European contact. Principal among these theories is that postulated by Jared Diamond in his book *Collapse: How Societies Choose to Fail or Survive*.

Mournful early drawing of the state of Rapa Nui

Diamond's saga of the decline and fall of Easter Island is straightforward and can be summarised in a few words: Within a few centuries after the island was settled, the people of Easter Island destroyed their forest, degraded the island's topsoil, wiped out their plants and drove their animals to extinction. As a result of this self-inflicted environmental devastation, its complex society collapsed, descending into civil war, cannibalism and self-destruction. When Europeans discovered the island in the 18th century, they found a crashed society and a deprived population of survivors who subsisted among the ruins of a once vibrant civilisation. (40)

While the theory of ecocide has become almost paradigmatic in environmental circles, a dark and gory secret hangs over the premise of Easter Island's self destruction: an actual genocide terminated Rapa Nui's indigenous populace and its culture. Diamond ignores, or neglects to address the true reasons behind Rapa Nui's collapse. Other researchers have no doubt that its people; their culture and its environment were destroyed to all intents and purposes by European slave-traders, whalers and colonists. After all, the cruelty and systematic kidnapping by European slave-merchants, the near-extermination of the Island's indigenous population and the deliberate destruction of the island's environment has been regarded as "one of the most hideous atrocities committed by white men in the South Seas" (41)

Unfortunately, most of the general public buy the overly simplistic idea that the Rapa Nui people defoliated their environment and then fell into a bitter civil war resulting in the wanton chopping down of the last tree in order to move the Moai. I sincerely hope that what you have gleaned from this book so far is that although human beings do have a tendency to alter their environments, the first Europeans on Rapa Nui did meet a prosperous and highly cultured civilization.

For example, there is new evidence that human beings may not have been responsible for the destruction after all. Although Easter Island has long been held to be the most important example of a traditional society destroying itself, it appears that the real culprits were rats - up to three million of them. (41b)

"A theme of self-inflicted, pre-European contact ecocide is common in published accounts," says the anthropologist Dr Terry Hunt, who led the research at the University of Hawaii. "Easter Island has become a paragon for prehistoric human-induced ecological catastrophe and cultural collapse." He has examined new data from the Hawaiian and other Pacific islands that shows that by early historic times the deforestation of Easter Island was already complete, or nearly so. A dense forest of palm trees and more than 20 other types of trees and shrubs had mostly disappeared. As many as six land birds and several seabirds had also become extinct.

The island had a relatively simple ecosystem with vegetation once dominated by millions of palms. The original ecosystem of the island, with a limited range of plants, and few if any predators, would, says the report, have been particularly vulnerable to alien invasions.

Almost all of the palm seed shells discovered on the island were found to have been gnawed by rats. Thousands of rat bones have been found, and crucially, much of the damage to forestry appears to have been done before evidence of fires on the island. (41c) And how would the rats have gotten there? Most likely as stowaways on vessels commanded by early visitors or migrants.

5000 horses on Rapa Nui continue the environmental destruction

8/ Making The Moai Walk

Experimental effort to make a Moai "walk"

Numerous attempts have been made to move the Moai from the quarry in Rano Raraku crater to their more commonplace present locations, in some cases a distance of 14 miles. Some suggest that they were moved in an upright position and kept stable by crews manning ropes. This mode would verify the island legends of the statues "walking" to their sites. From a distance seeing one of these great Moai moving along the road bobbing up and down as the logs moved underneath would surely have looked like a statue moving under its own power with a procession of people alongside it. (42)

However, recent computer simulations by Jo Anne von Tilburg at UCLA have shown that it would have been much simpler to position the Moai in a horizontal position on two large logs and then roll the whole unit along on other logs placed perpendicular to it. Using this method Van Tilburg calculated that an average Moai could have been moved from the quarry to Ahu Akivi in less than 5 days, using approximately 70 men. Her theories were recently put to the test in a successful experiment to move a Moai replica on Easter Island sponsored and filmed by Nova television in the United States.

Many Moai are still standing on the slopes of Rano Raraku volcano. These statues were still under construction when seemingly abandoned, as discussed earlier. They were carved on three sides, then lowered onto the slopes below where they were stood upright. Then the backs of the statues could be completed. Once that was done, they were then ready to be moved to their intended Ahu. But moving them was harder than carving them, and today many are still standing on the crater slopes.

The logistics involved must have been staggering. The Moai were lowered to the ground by ropes in order for the carving to be completed. Thus we find, on the very peak of the volcano rim, round holes carved into the rock, five feet deep and over two feet in diameter. Into these, the islanders would have placed palm trunks to act as bollards, and by running ropes around them they could control the statues as they lowered them down the 45 degree slope. It is calculated that the ropes must have been about 600 feet long and at least three inches thick.

Ropes were also used to move the Moai statues to the platforms. For this to work, the hauling ropes would have had to have been about 250 feet long, which at an inch thick would have weighed over a ton. Many people required to make the rope, many people required to pull. Some Moai were erected up to 15 miles from the quarry, and until recently it was assumed they would have been hauled along on wooden rollers. However, latest research by Professor Charles Love who has been excavating the Moai roads shows that rollers would not have worked because the road beds themselves were not level, but slightly concave. (43)

In 1986, Pavel Pavel, Thor Heyerdahl and the Kon Tiki Museum experimented with a five-ton Moai and a nine-ton Moai. With a rope around the head of the statue and another around the base, using eight workers for the smaller statue and 16 for the larger, they "walked" the Moai forward by swiveling and rocking it from side to side; however, the experiment was ended early due to damage to the statue bases from chipping. Despite the early end to the experiment, Thor

Heyerdahl estimated that this method for a 20-ton statue over Easter Island terrain would allow 320 feet (100 m) per day. (44)

Rather theatrical attempt to move a small Moai

And what do the oral traditions say? They speak of the use of Mana, a spiritual force which is well known throughout Polynesia. In Polynesian culture, Mana is a spiritual quality considered to have supernatural origin; a sacred impersonal force existing in the universe. Therefore to have Mana is to have influence and authority, and efficacy, the power to perform in a given situation. This essential quality of Mana is not limited to persons; peoples, governments, places and inanimate objects can possess Mana. There are different ways to obtain Mana: through birth, warfare and, according to Hawaiians, Pono (balanced) actions, reflecting the balance that exists in the world and humanity's responsibility toward maintaining that balance.. People or objects that possess Mana are accorded respect because their possession of Mana gives them authority, power, and prestige. The word's meaning is complex because Mana is a basic foundation of the Polynesian worldview.

The islanders have a legend that the statues were moved to the platforms and raised upright by the use of this Mana, or mind power. Either the god Make-

make, or priests or chiefs commanded them to walk or to float through the air, and according to one legend, use was made of a finely crafted stone sphere, 75 cm (2.5 ft) in diameter, called Te Pito Kura ('the golden navel' or 'the navel of light'), to focus the Mana. Legends about the use of levitation in the construction of megalithic monuments are found all over the world.

The face of Make Make

Some writers have said that high up on the rim inside the Rano Raraku crater is an open rock-hewn cave with a series of rock benches or seats lining its walls, oriented towards the crater lake. According to one tradition, seven masters, or magicians, sat together on the benches and combined their Mana to make the statues walk out of the crater and around the island in a clockwise spiral. (44b)

Francis Mazière was one of the few scholars to take the legends about Mana seriously:

'What if certain men at a certain period were able to make use of electro-magnetic or anti-gravitational forces? ... [O]n the sheer side of the volcano there is something wonderfully strange. Here statues were brought down over the top of dozens of others, without leaving any marks. Yet the movement of ten or twenty tons is by no means child's play. ...The natives say that everything died on Easter Island when mana left it, while at the same time I see the amazing evidence of a quite extraordinary past. It may be that para-psychology will find a sympathetic vibration in this island with its perturbed, confusing magnetism. (44c)

9/ Pukao: Red Hair Or Red Hats?

Pukao are the hats or topknots formerly placed on top of some moai statues on Easter Island. They were all carved from a very light red volcanic stone scoria, which was quarried from a single source at Puna Pau. Pukao are cylindrical in shape with a dent on the underside to fit on the head of the Moai and a boss or knot on top. They fitted onto the Moai in such a way that the Pukao protruded forwards. Their size varies in proportion to the Moai they were on but they can be up to 8 feet tall and 8 feet in diameter. But what are they?

Very little information is available as to what the Pukao is meant to portray. Throughout Polynesia, red was sacred color associated with both the deities and with the highest social classes. (45) This was especially true in Hawaii, where recreations of ceremonies performed by the Ali'i (Ariki in Tahiti) still occur to this day, though somewhat watered down once must admit.

Four Moai with Pukao at Anakena Beach

If the Pukao does represent a form of head ornament, then it would be unique to Rapa Nui, as such a shape is not seen in other Polynesian head gear. More likely the top knot represents the hair style of the elite of Rapa Nui. The colour, being red, could be the hairs' natural tone, or even possibly a dye of some kind, possibly ground lava, of the same stone that the Pukao were made from. However, why would they dye their hair red, as compared to another colour, or tone? Red is a colour of the nobility in much of "Polynesia," as is yellow, as seen in the painting below by Herb Kane. It seems far more likely to me that the red was used to imitate earlier people, of high class positions, who naturally had red hair.

Hawaiian painter Herb Kane's depiction of royalty

Again, from my 2012 trip to Rapa Nui I personally saw many individuals who had natural red coloured hair, and although many people would say that this was the result of Celtic or other European genetic infusion over the course of "post contact" times, the reddish shade is found, according to local informants, from one specific blood line, that of the Tuki family.

The Moai in the Rano Raraku quarry, as we have seen, tend to be the largest and the tops of the heads too narrow to wear a Pukao. It is also thought that these are the oldest of the sculptures, possibly predating the conventional arrival of the Polynesians. From this, one could surmise that the use of the Pukao was a Polynesian introduction, but this is simply speculation on the author's part.

The main Ahu at Anakena with restored Pukao

The above photo at Anakena Beach shows that the Moai needed to have great width and depth on the top of the head in order to secure the Pukao, which often weighed tons. Also, these Moai would all had had the coral and red scoria eyes at one time. However, those at Rano Raraku tend to have less surface area on the top, and I personally saw no evidence of fallen Pukao in the area.

A cluster of Moai on the outer area of Rano Raraku

The lack of Pukao at Rano Raraku could be because, according to conventional archaeology, none of them were actually finished, but a curious thing about many of them is that they never seem to have been made to accept the eyes as described in the above text. For myself, this indicates two completely distinct styles of design, and perhaps two completely different building periods, with the Rano Raraku ones being the older of the two.

All of the Pukao have come from a very specific quarry called Puna Pau, which is close to Hangaroa. In the photo below you can see that the large red top knots were sculpted into a round shape prior to their movement to specific Moai. This allowed them to be rolled, rather than carried or dragged.

Roughed out Pukao inside the Puna Pau quarry

Pukao with core removed to fit on protrusion on the Moai's head

10/ Rongorongo: The Only Polynesian Text?

In 1864, the French lay missionary Eugène Eyraud , the first known non-Polynesian resident of Earth's most isolated inhabited island, Rapa Nui, reported in a letter to his superior that he had seen there "in all the houses" hundreds of tablets and staffs incised with thousands of hieroglyphic figures. Two years later, only a small handful of these incised artefacts were left. Most Rongorongo, as the unique objects were subsequently called, had by then been burnt, hidden away in caves, or deftly cannibalized for boat planks, fishing lines, or honorific skeins of human hair. The few Rapanui survivors of recent slave raids and contagions evidently no longer feared the objects' erstwhile Tapu or sacred prohibition.

When Eugène Eyraud died of tuberculosis on Rapanui four years later in 1868, his fellow missionaries there, who had arrived only in 1866, knew nothing of the existence of incised tablets and staffs on the island. Rongorongo comprised the Easter Islanders' best-kept secret. (46)

One of the few Rongorongo tablets that remain

The glyphs contain about 120 basic elements, but these are combined to form between 1500 and 2000 compound signs. Many of the motifs are also found in the island's rock art, but none are found on any statues or platforms.

The precise nature of the Rongorongo script is uncertain. The prevailing view today is that 'the motifs represent a rudimentary phonetic writing system, in which picture symbols were used to express ideas as well as objects. In other words, the individual glyphs do not represent an alphabet or even syllables, as in other scripts, but are 'cue cards' for whole words or ideas, plus a means of keeping count, like rosary beads. Each sign was a peg on which to hang a large amount of text committed to memory.' (46b)

According to legend, Hoto Matua brought 67 Rongorongo tablets with him containing traditions, genealogical tables, and other records of the past, and he was accompanied by learned men who knew the art of writing and reciting the inscriptions. Some researchers have argued that the Tongorongo script is not ancient but was invented by the islanders after the Spanish visit in 1770, when a written proclamation of annexation was offered to the chiefs and priests for them to sign. Some of the symbols used by the natives in signing the proclamation resembled the Rongorongo hieroglyphs. It's possible that all the existing Rongorongo tablets are no more than a few hundred years old; one, for instance, consists of a European oar. But the inscriptions could have been copied from earlier specimens.

The last truly literate islanders died either as a result of the 1862 slave raid or the subsequent smallpox epidemic. Natives who later claimed to be able to read Rongorongo appeared to be either reciting memorized texts or merely describing the figures rather than actually reading them, and sometimes gave different renderings of the same text. The script has still not been deciphered, despite claims to have done so. In 1995, for example, Steven Fischer announced that most of the tablets were religious chants taking the form: god A copulated with goddess B begetting a particular animal, plant, or natural phenomenon. However, his claims to have deciphered the script have been roundly attacked by other researchers. (46c)

No other Polynesian culture had a hieroglyphic system, so why do we find it on Rapa Nui? Many scholars have argued that the origins of this form of writing can be found in various parts of the world, from ancient India to Central and South America, yet no coherent ties have been proven. Most of Rapa Nui's Rongorongo inscriptions consist of parallel lines of signs or glyphs that represent human figures, birds, fishes, plants, geometrics, and other things. These fingernail-size glyphs were traditionally incised on large battle staffs, driftwood tablets, small wooden "Birdmen" and other statuettes, pectorals, ceremonial paddles, and even human skulls. Rongorongo glyphs also figured among the inventory of special tattoos for the Rongorongo experts. On the staffs and tablets, every other line of Rongorongo appears upside down; this orientation forces the reader to rotate the artefact 180 degrees at the end of each line of glyphs, evidently to enable continuous reading and to avoid confusing the parallel lines. At a cursory glance, Rongorongo offers a fanciful parade of hieroglyphics, and for over 130 years many eminent scholars from many nations have burned the midnight oil in attempting to discover what this hieroglyphic parade celebrates.

Conventional researchers believe that the Rongorongo script is Polynesian, with its signs reflecting the local environment and culture. Some see far more significant similarities between certain Rongorongo motifs and designs employed in the Solomon Islands in Melanesia, though a direct migration from there to Easter Island is no longer considered tenable. Rongorongo specialist Thomas Barthel speculated that the script originated on the Polynesian islands of Huahine or Raiatea and he believed it came to Rapa Nui with Hotu Matu'a.

Rongorongo is often said to be the first script to be found in Oceania. However, in 1913 John Macmillan Brown found a script of some 60 characters on Woleai Atoll in the Caroline Islands. Whereas the Easter Island script is largely ideographic, the Woleai script was syllabic, but unlike any other in the world. It was used by the young chief of the island and was known only to five people on it, though it was also in use on Faraulep, a small island about 160 km to the northeast. In 1908 an expedition to Faraulep collected a number of symbols forming part of a counting system. The numbers ranged from 100,000 to 60 million and would have had no use in daily life. It seems unlikely that the Woleai script originated on a small isolated island. (46d)

Script itself is a non-Polynesian characteristic and the search for its origin was eventually rewarded through one of its particular characteristics, which is that it is 'arranged in boustrophedon, i.e. in a continuous serpentine band where every second line is turned upside-down. Europeans, Chinese and the Indus Valley people never wrote in boustrophedon, and the language had been forgotten by the time of the Europeans first arrival. In fact, the only place in the world where this particular style of writing can be found is in South America; Peru to be precise. (47)

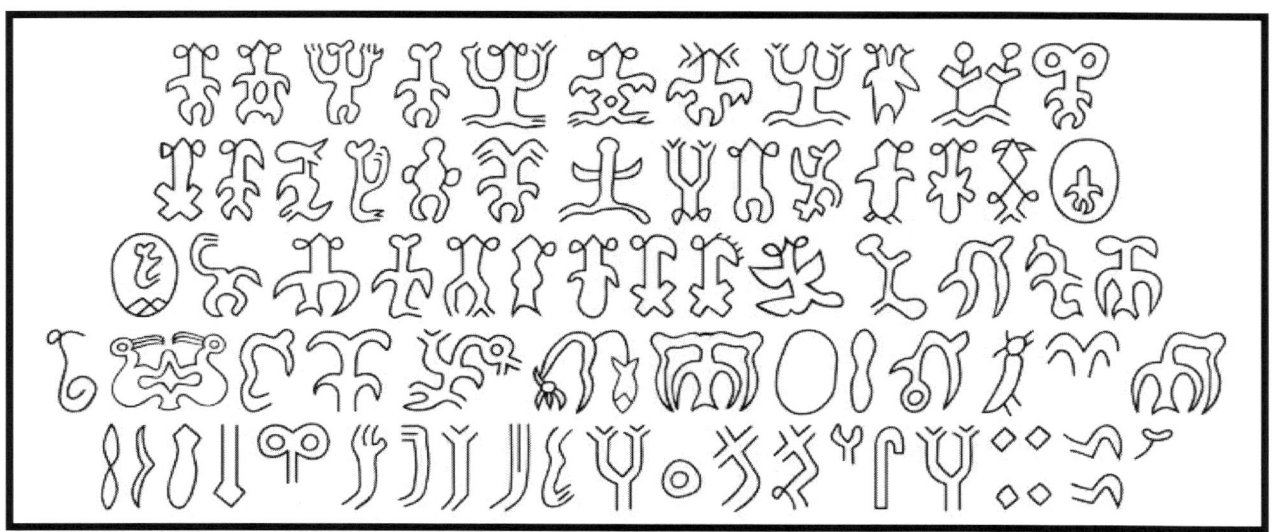

Detail of Rongorongo

Most researchers acknowledge that boustrophedon was used in Peru but say that there is no affinity between the signs used in the two places, though there might have been some influence in either direction.

Heyerdahl mentions that on the arrival of the Europeans, the Indians of Lake Titicaca area still '*continued a primitive form of picture writing.*' (48) This conforms with the observation by Russian Rongorongo expert J. V. Knorozov, that the only two places where 'reversed boustrophedon' occur in the world are Easter Island and ancient Peru. Sariemento Gamboa, famous Inca chronicler, upon consulting an assembly of forty-two learned Inca historians recorded the following in reference to the ninth Inca Patchacuti Inca Yupanqui:

'...after he had well ascertained the most notable of their ancient histories he had it all painted after its order on large boards, and he placed them in the house of the sun, where the said boards, which were garnished with gold, would be like our libraries, and he appointed learned men who could understand and explain them...' (49)

The famous Pachacutec Inca Yupanqui, who was in fact the 10th high ruling Inca, reigned from 1438 to 1472. Fernando de Montesinos was a writer from Spain, who lived in Peru, and published a book entitled "The Historical Memoirs Of Peru" in 1644, in which he states, based on another book called The Quito Manuscript, by an earlier unknown writer, that the Inca had a written, or more correctly, a hieroglyphic language. This was called Qillqa, and The Quito Manuscript states:

"The amautas (learned men) say that the events of those times were known by the traditions of the most ancient ones...that when this prince reigned (Pachacutec) there were letters, and men learned in them, whom they call amautas, and these taught reading and writing."

Pachacutec is believed to have banned the use of this writing system, and had all examples of it burned. There does however, remain tantalizing evidence that examples of this hieroglyphic system may still exist. A few tapestries and tunics worn by the royal Inca which still exist portray repeating patterns of specific symbols.

What informants on Rapa Nui told me is that some of them still know how to read and write in Rongorongo, and the reason they have remained quiet about this is due to the sacred nature of the messages in the writing, which they believe belongs exclusively to them. Also, each symbol cannot be directly translated into any other known language, because the symbols convey different layers of meaning, depending upon the intent of their use, and which other symbols are placed in association with them.

The Rapa Nui people I spoke with guard the knowledge which they still carry fiercely, but secretly. Since their population was so grossly decimated from the very moment that "first contact" was made with Roggeveen in 1722, through recent scuffles with the Chilean government to the present day, that which they deem sacred, and not discovered or shared with outsiders may well remain so into the distant future. Rongorongo's messages still speak to the people of Rapa Nui, and may well only continue to do so within a tight, trusted circle of wisdom keepers. Can you blame them for doing so?

Also, their reasoning, to some extent, as to why the other Pacific Islands of the Maohi world do not have Rongorongo or an equivalent, is because the people of knowledge of that island chose not to allow it to be dispersed, as they claim they are the source and root of the Maohi people. Were other island people not worthy to learn of and carry the knowledge? We may never be privy to know.

11/ Non Polynesian DNA Prior To Europeans?

So, did South Americans help colonise Easter Island centuries before Europeans reached it? Clear genetic evidence has, for the first time, given support to elements of this controversial theory showing that while the remote island was mostly colonised from the west, as in Polynesia, there was also some influx of people from the Americas.

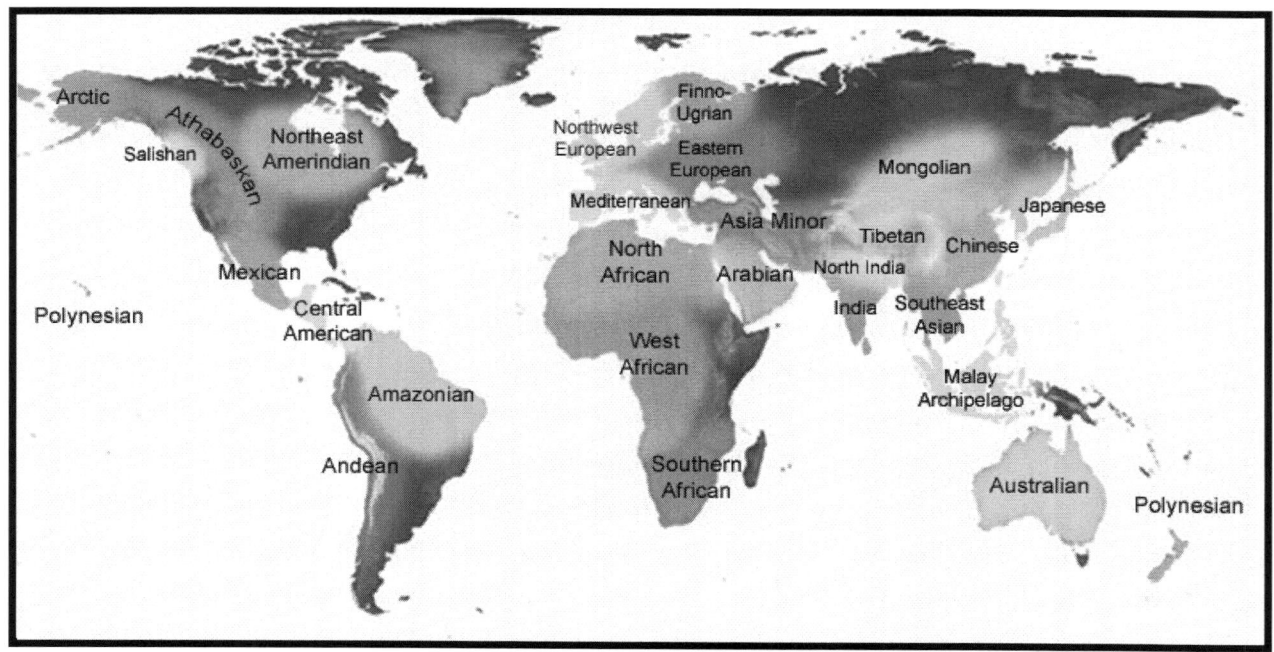

Basic map of global genetic groups

Erik Thorsby of the University of Oslo in Norway has found clear evidence to support elements of Heyerdahl's hypothesis. In 1971 and 2008 he collected blood samples from Easter Islanders whose ancestors had not interbred with Europeans and other visitors to the island. Thorsby looked at the HLA genes, which vary greatly from person to person. Most of the islanders' HLA genes were Polynesian, but a few of them also carried HLA genes only previously found in Native American populations. (50)

Because most of Thorsby's volunteers came from one extended family, he was able to work out when the HLA genes entered their lineage. The most probable first known carrier was a woman named Maria Aquala, born in 1846. Crucially, that was before the slave traders arrived in the 1860s and began interbreeding with the islanders.

But the genes may have been around for longer than that. Thorsby found that in some cases the Polynesian and American HLA genes were shuffled together, the result of a process known "recombination". This is rare in HLA genes, meaning the

American genes would need to be around for a certain amount of time for it to happen. Thorsby can't put a precise date on it, but says it is likely that Americans reached Easter Island before it was "discovered" by Europeans in 1722.

This does not completely solve the riddle of the possible arrival of migrants from the coast of the Americas, and most likely Peru as we have seen, but it adds real genetic, and thus concrete scientific evidence that will fuel future investigations.

The Important Archaeological Sites

12/ Vinapu

The Ahu of Vinapu is a relatively large site, located on the southeast corner of Rapa Nui, just in front of the approach to the airport runway. The Ahu exhibits extraordinary stonemasonry consisting of large, carefully fitted slabs of dense basalt. The American archaeologist, William Mulloy investigated the site in 1958. (51)

The very tight fitting basalt stones of Vinapu

According to the thesis of Jean Hervé Daude, Ahu Vinapu was built by the Inca Tupac Yupanqui during his expedition to the Pacific in 1465. (52) The Chullpa of Sillustani in the Andes, regarded by most archaeologists as having been built under the reign of the Inca Tupac Yupanqui, are eerily similar as regards tight fitting construction techniques as Ahu Vinapu, and hence the theory that Tupac Yupanqui was responsible for building both.

However, there is no actual proof that any of the Inca built the finest of the Chullpa at Sillustani. It is more likely that such structures predate the Inca and any other known civilization of the area, crafted by an as yet unnamed civilization that had much more advanced tools than the bronze chisels and stone hammers of the Inca and others. It is therefore possible that Ahu Vinapu also predates the majority of Ahu and other sites on Rapanui, and was perhaps made by the same or a similar culture as that seen in Peru.

Tight and mortar free basalt stones of Sillustani

Most of the Ahu and other stone structures on Rapa Nui are composed of somewhat roughly shaped basalt stone blocks and volcanic stone fill, similar to many found in other Polynesian locations like Hawaii, Tahiti and the Cook Islands. What sets Ahu Vinapu and a few of the other sites apart from these is the level of stone shaping refinement.

The finest platform masonry, such as that found at Ahu Tahiri (one of the two Ahu at Vinapu), consists of 'enormous squared and tooled stones, that turn the edge of the toughest modern steel'. (53) The best facade slabs commonly weigh 2 or 3 tons. At Vinapu one of the polished basalt slabs measures 2.5 by 1.7 m (8 by 5.5

ft) and weighs 6 or 7 tons. According to John MacMillan Brown, who is quoted above from his book "The Riddle Of The Pacific" he goes on to say:

'The colossal blocks are tooled and cut so as to fit each other. In the Ahu Vinapu and in the fragment of the ahu near Hangaroa beach the stones are as colossal as in the old Temple of the Sun in Cuzco, they are as carefully tooled, and the irregularities of their sides that have to come together are so cut that the two faces exactly fit into each other. These blocks are too huge to have been shifted frequently to let the mason find out whether they fitted or not. They must have been cut and tooled to exact measurement or plan. There is no evidence of chipping after they have been laid. Every angle and projection must have been measured with scientific precision before the stones were nearing their finish.' (54)

There are signs of different stages of Ahu construction at Vinapu. Detailed examinations during Heyerdahl's first expedition led to the conclusion that 'Vinapu 1' or Tahiri (the structure with the classical stone masonry) belonged to the earliest building period (which in Heyerdahl's view still meant the 8th century AD), contrary to all previous theories, and that the platform had twice been rebuilt and added to by far less capable architects. (55)

This is clearly the case in Cusco and surrounding areas of Peru, as well as Egypt. Often the lower works in stone are not only comprised of the largest stones, but also the finest in terms of execution. In the case of the Ahu Tahiri section of Ahu Vinapu, the central lower wall section is the most precise, while the areas to the right and left, which give strong indications of repair and reassembly, are poorer, and probably of later execution.

To those readers that feel that there is a sense of racism in the above observations, that is clearly not the intent, from me at least. What it simply seems to show is that an earlier people existed on Rapa Nui who had tool technology and knowledge not seemingly present during the times and of the people we commonly call Polynesian.

Left and right sections of Ahu Tahiri are inferior to the central part

The official position is that all Easter Island's platforms are simply variations of the Marae platforms of central and eastern Polynesia, which were socio-religious centers and shrines to ancestral gods. Vinapu's megalithic stone wall is said to bear only a superficial resemblance to the classic 'Incan' masonry because, unlike the solid block construction used in Peru, the Easter Island walls are merely a facing of slabs that mask a rubble core.

However, there are also striking similarities with the pre-Incan Andean style of masonry. Each slab is convex or pillow-shaped, with slightly beveled edges, and stones with projecting edges are fitted into stones with receding edges. The blocks are irregularly shaped, fit together with the utmost precision, and small holes or chinks are filled with perfectly fitted stones.

A block in one corner of the Vinapu wall has a projecting knob – just like many large blocks in Peru. The corners of the seawall are rounded, and its entire face is in fact slightly convex, again as in the Andes. Prof. Camila Laureani, a connoisseur of Tiwanaku (Tiahuanaco Bolivia) and 'Inca'-type masonry writes:

'Ahu Vinapu is an architectonic construction which combines the essential characteristics of the structures in the Altiplano of Peru-Bolivia in a manner so evident that one cannot doubt the arrival on the island of a contingent of these people.' (56)

13/ Orongo

Orongo is a stone village and ceremonial centre at the southwestern tip of Rapa Nui, on the edge of the large water filled crater called Rano Kau. The first half of the ceremonial village's 53 stone masonry houses were investigated and restored in 1974 by American archaeologist William Mulloy. In 1976 Mulloy assisted by Chilean archaeologists Claudio Cristino and Patricia Vargas completed the restoration of the whole complex which was subsequently investigated by Cristino in 1985 and 1995. 'Orongo enjoys a dramatic location on the crater lip of Rano Kau at the point where a 250 meter sea cliff converges with the inner wall of the crater.' (57)

Looking inside Rano Kau crater with totora reeds growing

Until the mid-nineteenth century, Orongo was the centre of the birdman cult, which hosted an annual race to bring the first manutara (Sooty Tern) egg from the islet of Motu Nui to Orongo. The site has numerous petroglyphs, mainly of tangata manu (birdmen). In the 1860s, most of the Rapa Nui islanders died of disease or were enslaved, and when the survivors were converted to Christianity, Orongo fell into disuse.

Afew mof the many Birdman glyphs to be seen at Orongo

A paramount chief, called the Ariki Mau held the original power in the society, as was typical throughout Polynesia. Over time, the chief's omnipotence declined (possibly as a result of ecological stresses), and the secular power on the island was seized by a warrior class, called Matatoa, whose emblem was the Birdman. The result was a decline in the old religion of ancestor worship and an increase in acts of warfare. At this time, statue making appears to have ceased, and the birdman cult came into being. (58) Many sources believe that this transition happened sometime in the 16th century AD.

The most sacred area at Orongo is called Mata Ngarau, where priests chanted and prayed for success in the annual birdman egg hunt. This was a contest to obtain the first egg of the season from the offshore islet Motu Nui, the outermost of three small islands. Contestants descended the sheer cliffs of Orongo and swam to Motu Nui where they awaited the coming of the birds. Having procured an egg, the contestant swam back and presented it to his sponsor, who then was declared birdman for that year, an important status position.

The island of Motu Nui in the background

In the Rapa Nui mythology, the deity Make-make was the chief god of the birdman cult, the other three gods associated with it being Hawa-tuu-take-take (the Chief of the eggs) his wife Vie Hoa and Vie Kanatea. Contestants were revealed in dreams by ivi-attuas (individuals with the gift of prophecy). The contestants would each appoint a Hopu who would swim to Motu Nui and fetch them the Egg, whilst the contestants waited at Orongo. The race was very dangerous and many Hopu were killed by sharks, drowning or by falling. (59)

Once the first egg was collected, the final task would be for the unsuccessful contestants to return to Orongo, the winner allowed to remain in Motu Nui until he felt spiritually prepared to return. On his return he would present the egg to his patron, who had already shaved his head and painted it either white or red. The successful man would be declared Tangata Manu, would take the egg in his hand and lead a procession down the slope of Rano Kau and on either to Anakena Beach (on the northwest side of the island) if he was from the western clans or Rano Raraku (the Moai quarry on the eastern side) if he was from the eastern clans.

Once in residence there he was Tapu (sacred) for the next five months of his year-long status, and allowed his nails to grow and wore a headdress of human hair. The new Tangata Manu was given a new name, entitled to gifts of food and other tributes (including his clan having sole rights to collect that season's harvest of wild bird eggs and fledglings from Motu Nui), and went into seclusion for a year in a special ceremonial house. (60)

Researchers such as Dr. Robert Schoch, the Boston University geologist find the stone houses at Orongo intriguing, and question their original purpose. I visited the site with Dr. Schoch in November of 2012, and he observed that the basalt slabs which made up these low stone buildings were very carefully fitted together. Made so as a defensive strategy against human attack? Highly unlikely.

His treatise, covered extensively in "Forgotten Civilization: The Role of Solar Outbursts in Our Past and Future," published in 2012 and available via www.amazon.com as well as his website www.robertschoch.com carefully lays out a curious explanation. In the past, powerful plasma events sometimes took place, due to solar outbursts and coronal mass ejections (CMEs) from the Sun, or possibly emissions from other celestial objects. Powerful plasma phenomena could cause strong electrical discharges to hit Earth, burning and incinerating materials on our planet's surface.

It is his assertion that such an event, global in scale and resulting in the very rapid melting of the polar ice caps around 9700 BC and thus ending the Ice Age and raising sea levels by about 350 feet could have caused later generations to build seemingly fortified stone structures to ward off the repeat of such a catastrophe.

One of the many low stone buildings at Orongo called Hare Moa

A real bone of contention for the present day population of Rapa Nui is the presence of a basalt stone Moai presently on display at the British Museum in London, England. It is called Hoa Hakanani'a, from the Rapa Nui language, and has been interpreted as meaning "stolen or hidden friend" (61) or perhaps "Master Wave Breaker." (62) It was "removed" from Orongo on 7 November 1868 by the crew of the English ship HMS Topaze, and arrived in Portsmouth on 25 August 1869.

I chose to put the word removed in parentheses because that is clearly what one would call a politically correct term. In reality, the Moai was stolen, and donated to the British Museum by Queen Victoria. What is intriguing about Hoa Hakanani'a is that it is made of dense basalt. Approximately 10 Moai exist composed of this type of stone, while the other approximately 900 are made of volcanic tuff, which is basically compressed ash.

Hoa Hakanani'a in the British Museum

Basalt is far harder to shape than is tuff, and since the densest material available for making tools which could have been used to shape the Moai is also basalt, how could Hoa Hakanani'a have been made? The few surviving basalt Moai have been found at deeper stratigraphic levels below other Moai and the platforms upon which they were erected, or were reused in later structures. Thus indicating the basalt Moai are among the earliest on the island. (63)

Another major puzzle, which is directly applicable to the chronology and dating of the Moai, is the matter of where they were quarried. Quarries on the rim of the volcanic crater, where large Moai were carved from the volcanic tuffs, are well exposed and still contain partially carved Moai in place. However, the quarries where the few basalt Moai were carved have never been definitively located, despite the small size of the island. Based on the geology of Rapa Nui, Dr. Schoch expects that any suitable basalt deposits would occur lower in the stratigraphic section, so low in fact that they might currently be under sea level off the coast of the island. That is, the basalt quarries might be under water. What Schoch is intimating is that the basalt Moai may have been originally carved prior to the end of the last Ice Age...

The supposed place at Rano Kau where Hoa Hakanani'a once stood

14/ Rano Raraku

View of Rano Raraku from a distance

Pierre Loti, who visited Easter Island in 1872, assigned the statues standing at Rano Raraku to a very early period:

'They are the work of less childish artists who knew how to give them an expression. They frighten. ... What human race do they represent, with their pointed noses and their thin lips that show a pout of disdain or mockery? ... According to the tradition conserved by the old people they were earlier than the arrival of their own ancestors. The migrants from Polynesia ... found the island deserted, guarded only by these monstrous visages. ... Gnawed by lichens they seem to have the patina of fifty centuries like our celtic menhirs.' (63b)

Francis Mazière, too, distinguishes between two periods of sculpture. He believed that many of the statues at Rano Raraku, including nearly all the raised statues at the foot of the volcano, belonged to the first period. During a huge excavation at

Rano Raraku, he uncovered two 10 meter statues, undamaged by erosion, which were completely white and very highly polished. The wings of the nose and the trace of the muscles in the upper lip were handled with striking delicacy and technical skill. Their elegant hands, joined at the height of the navel, in a meditating posture, ended in prodigiously long, tapering nails. The top of their heads was very narrow and clearly not designed for a cylindrical red hat. More such statues were subsequently uncovered. There are also marked differences among the Rano Raraku statues themselves: in general, the statues inside the crater are smaller and less carefully made than those on the outer slope.

Rano Raraku is one of two major quarry sites on Easter Island (Rapa Nui), where the large Moai were carved out of the distinctive yellow-brown volcanic tuff. Both Rano Raraku on the east side of the island and Puna Pau on the west are quarries made of geologically dormant volcanic cones. (64)

Approaching the quarry area outside the Rano Rarako crater

Rano Raraku is a volcanic cone with a steep exterior slope and a hollow interior. Several quarry areas are carved into the exterior and interior of the cone, and approximately 160 Moai still lie within the quarries, at least partly shaped. The quarry itself is not a massive excavation, but rather numerous separate quarry areas, cut and carved into the cone separately, and perhaps by separate villages or groups.

Radially extending out from Rano Raraku are several dressed roads, some with kerbstones. Although the roads were first identified in the 1910s by Katherine Routledge, archaeologist and author of the book "The Mystery of Easter Island" published in 1919, at first few scholars accepted the interpretations of Routledge's features as roads. The roads were first excavated by Charles Love nearly a hundred years later. Love found that the roads appear to be U-shaped in cross-section, rather than flat, supporting Routledge's assertion that the purpose of these roads was to move Moai from Rano Raraku to their final place of erection. A ritual function of the shape of these roads, and of course, of everything associated with Moai carving, is certain to have been important. (65)

View from Rano Raraku looking towards the ocean

On my visit in November of 2012, our driver/guide told us that during the excavations by Charles Love beautiful and tight fitting paving stones were found to make up the roads, but had to soon be covered up because the local people were extracting them for house building material.

Based on the evidence from the quarries, much of the Moai form was carved while the rock was in place, and generally they were carved out as if they were lying in on their backs. Then the Moai were detached from the parent rock, moved to the lower slopes and pushed erect, where the carving on the backs of the Moai was completed. Finally, the Moai were moved from the quarry along one of several roads to the places where they were to be erected permanently.

The largest of all Moai, unfinished and estimated at about 200 tons

Whether the 160 or so Moai left in place at the quarry were "unfinished" or not has been a point of contention among scholars as yet today. At least some of the statues at Rano Raraku were cut completely out of the quarry rock and erected onto platforms. They look unfinished, because they were buried by later quarry debris, sometimes up to their necks, but in fact, this may not be the case.

Again, referring to the work of Dr. Robert Schoch, a PhD in geology, The levels of sedimentation around certain Moai also impressed him. Some Moai have been buried in up to an estimated six meters (20 feet) of sediment, or more, such that even though they are standing erect, only their chins and heads are above the current ground level. Such high levels of sedimentation could occur quickly, for instance, if there were catastrophic landslides or mudflows, but Schoch could not find any such evidence (and landslides would tend to shift and knock over the tall statues). Rather, to his eye, the sedimentation around certain Moai suggests a much more extreme antiquity than most conventional archaeologists and historians believe to be the case.

Not only does sedimentation around the statues suggest a longer and different chronology than conventionally accepted, but so too do weathering and erosion patterns, and stylistic considerations. Although on one level most of the Moai are stylistically similar and even stereotypic, at another level each is unique and they could, Schoch believes, be categorized according to stylistic considerations. (66)

15/ Ahu Tongariki

Ahu Tongariki is the largest Ahu on Rapa Nui. Its Moai were toppled during the island's civil wars and in the twentieth century the Ahu was swept inland by a tsunami. It has since been restored and has fifteen Moai including an 86 tonne one that was the heaviest ever erected on the island. Ahu Tongariki is one kilometer northwest from Rano Raraku.

Another view of Ahu Tongariki

16/ Ahu Tahai

Situated near the town of Hanga Roa, the Ahu at Tahai sits near a canoe ramp made of rounded beach stones, and was restored by the American archaeologist William Mulloy. Ahu Tahai is thought to be among the earliest Ahu structures on the island, dating back to AD 690. (67) Not a single complex, Tahai comprises three principal Ahu from north to south: Ko Te Riku (with restored eyes), Tahai, and Vai Ure.

View from near Ko Te Riku

What is also found here are the Hare Moa (literal translation is chicken house) that are more numerous, and discussed in regards to Orongo. While those at Orongo are associated, by some scholars to relate directly to the Bird Man competition, the openings at Ahu Tahai are more ambiguous.

Another feature are the foundation remains of houses shaped in the form of overturned boats. They are called Hare Paenga and had a single door in the middle of one side. The foundation stones of these elliptical houses were made of cut basalt. To make the pointed ends the right shape, the blocks had to be hewn to the correct curvature. The stones measure 0.5 to 2.5 meters long, 20 or 30 centimeters wide, and at least 50 centimeters high; the largest weigh up to 10 tonnes. Small holes were bored in their upper surfaces, into which the islanders inserted thin branches to support the arched reed roof. The dwellings varied enormously in size; some could house more than 100 people, but others only half a dozen. (68)

Finely restored Hare Paenga at Ahu Tahai

Though found at many sites on Rapa Nui, the one in the above photo at Ahu Tahai is one of the best examples still existing.

But were the Paenga stones originally intended for the foundations of thatched houses? As author John Macmillan Brown said: 'The timbers of their houses look ridiculous alongside the cyclopean stone-foundations, into the small holes in which they were stuck.' The stones are of the hardest basalt, tooled to perfection, and 'were evidently intended by their original architects to bear the framework of great structures'. He also says: 'It is difficult to understand how they bored the inch-deep holes for the wooden posts in the adamantine basalt of the foundation stones.' (69)

17/ Puna Pau

Puna Pau is a quarry in a small crater or cinder cone on the outskirts of Hanga Roa in the south west of Rapa Nui, and the source for the red scoria that the Rapanui used to carve the Pukao (topknots) that they put on the heads of some of their iconic Moai statues. The stone from Puna Pau was also used for a few non-standard Moai and also for some petroglyphs.

Two of the unfinished Pukao at Puna Pau

The average Pukao was 2.4 meters high, 1.5 meters in diameter and weighed 5 tonnes, while the heaviest weighed 12 tonnes. It appears that they were added to Moai using a ramp of small stones, after the Moai were erected.

Source of the red scoria for the Pukao

18/ Anakena

The beach at Anakena

Anakena is the larger of the only two bays with truly sandy beaches on Rapa Nui. It is also known as Hanga Rau O Te 'Ariki, The Bay Of The King, named after Hotu Matu'a, who supposedly disembarked here upon his arrival to the island. The king's first house is also said to have been here. Anakena has two Ahu. One is called Ahu Ature Huke and has only one Moai. The other is often called Ahu Nau Na (also spelled Nao Nao) and has seven Moai, two of which are deteriorated.

The legends of Easter Island say that Hotu Matu'a first came ashore here and that this was the island's first settlement. Excavations of the site have confirmed that it had been occupied for a very long time. The current Ahu Nau Nau is built upon the remains of several others and the same precise stone work is found in the buried Ahu as that of Ahu Vinapu. Again, this is curious because one would expect the more advanced stonework work have been done during later periods of the island's development.

Section of a Hare Paenga reused in Ahu Nau Nau

The statues at Ahu Nau Nau are also known for the detailed carvings on their backs. Along with traditional loin cloth reliefs are fishhook patterns that are found on none of the other statues.

The detail work in the statues at Ahu Nau Nau is truly remarkable. Precisely chiseled facial features, the now familiar long ears and thin lips are all carved on the Ahu Nau Nau statues to a degree not seen at other sites. Although, not the biggest of the Moai, they are clearly the most refined. A fitting tribute if this is, indeed, the site of Rapa Nui's first settlement.

Finely carved back of one of the Moai

It was at Anakena that one of the island's secrets was finally discovered. Archeologist long puzzled over the deep eye sockets of the Moai that had been erected. Could it be that the Moai had in fact had eyes? In 1978, a student named Sonia Haoa found fragments of worked coral and a red disk made out of scoria, the same material used to make the Pukao. When fitted together they made an unmistakable eye. She brought the fragments to archeologist Segio Rapu who discovered they fit precisely in the eye socket of a Moai. So, the Moai did have eyes, although, it is unclear if they were permanent fixtures of the statues or placed in them only on ceremonial occasions as is done now on the island with replicas of the eyes.

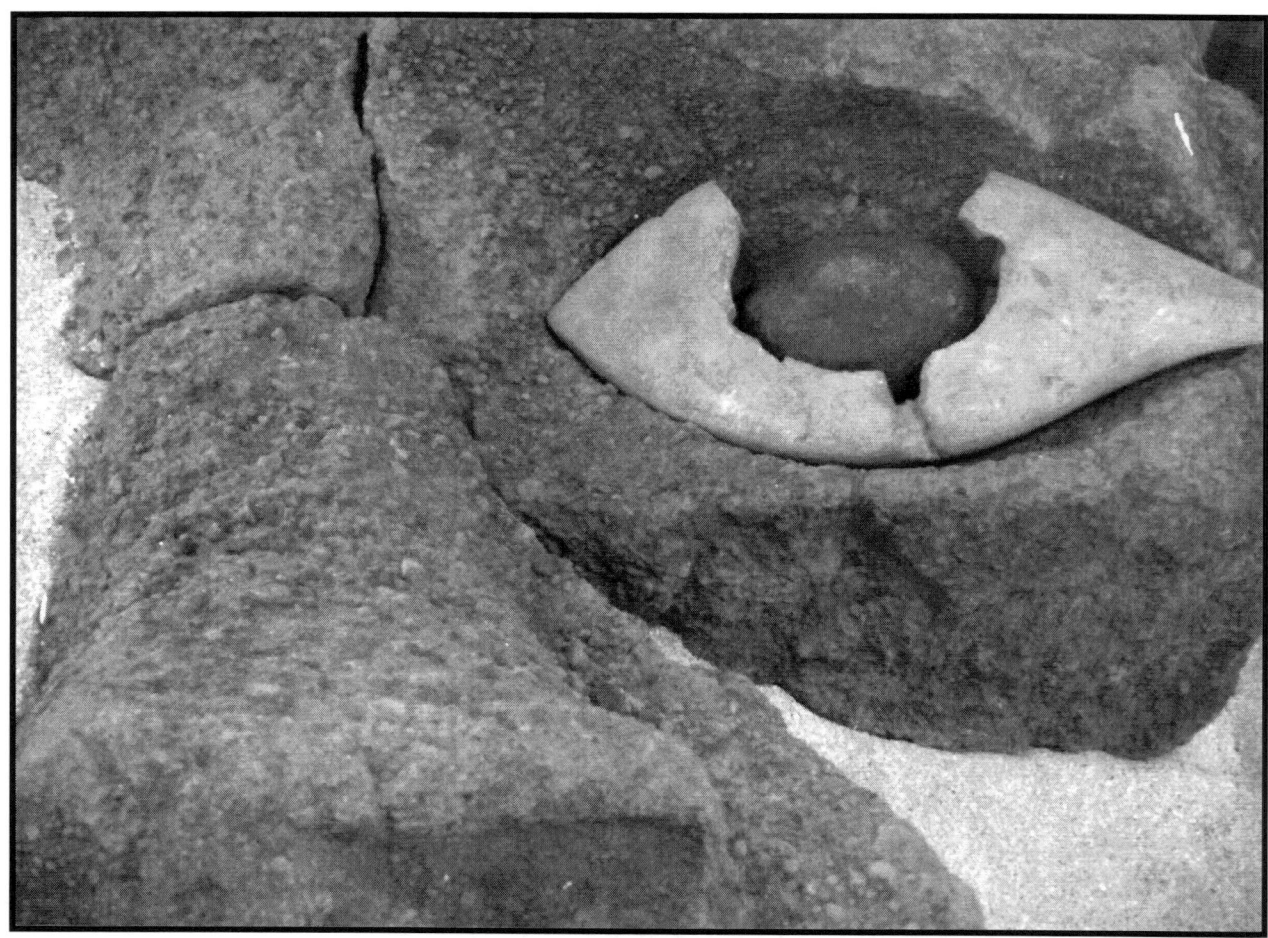

Reconstructed eye at the local museum

During Heyerdahl's expedition in 1987, excavations were carried out on the landward side of Ahu Nau Nau. A neatly fitted pavement made of boulders was found 7 ft below the surface. Three feet below it, a layer of soil full of human refuse was found, which was radiocarbon dated to AD 850. Trenches sunk along the landward side also uncovered a beautiful wall of megalithic slabs, perfectly hewn and fitted. According to Heyerdahl, this type of masonry was unmistakably an Early Period product that had been buried in silt before the Middle Period Ahu was erected. A closer inspection proved that these fine slabs had been part of an even older structure originally existing elsewhere, one that had been dismantled by man or destroyed by nature. The slabs had been dragged to this place from another site, and although perfectly polished and joined in the original wall, they had then been reworked to fit them together according to another plan.

Thor Heyerdahl inspecting excavations at Ahu Nau Nau

This discovery demolished the popular theory that such walls had appeared at a late stage on Easter Island and represented the high peak of local evolution due to the lack of timber. This buried wall was clearly older than the Middle Period walls visible above ground. Nothing like it has been found on a single island in the whole of Polynesia, but it is typical of the megalithic walls of South America. (71)

19/ Ahu Te Pito Kura

The stones of Te Pito Kura

This site, relatively close to Anakena, and by the sea has two main features. Here we find the largest Moai that was ever moved, and a small circle of stones which had and has great spiritual importance. The Rapa Nui term "Te Pito Kura" translates to "Golden Navel", or "Navel of Light", while "Te Pito Te Henua" means "Navel of the World"; which is what Rapa Nui is often referred to by its residents. This specific site is the navel of the navel, as it were. Stone barriers surround a worked stone sphere (the "navel" itself) measuring some 75 centimeters in diameter, reputedly brought by founder Hotu Matu'a from overseas. Geological sourcing, however, indicates the sphere is actually of local origin.

Some of the islanders believe, according to oral tradition that the central stone was used as an energy focusing device and assisted, somehow in the movement of the Moai.

The Ahu next to Te Pito Kura also has the largest moai (Paro, standing 9.8 meters tall at 82 tonnes, with an 11.5 tonne Pukao) known to have been ever erected on an Ahu; toppled sometime after 1838, it was one of the last (if not the last) standing Moai on the island until modern times. (72)

The massive toppled Moai called Paro

20/ Ahu Akivi

This site is likely most famous for the fact that the seven Moai on the Ahu all face the ocean, whereas most Moai look inland. Also, it is the only major Ahu which is not located in close proximity to the sea.

The Seven Navigators

The most common story regarding the Moai here are that they represent the seven navigators sent by Hotu Matu'a to find a new home land. Their position has them facing directly at the sunset during Spring and Autumn Equinox; and have their backs to the sunrise during Spring and Autumn Equinox.

Although many visitors assume the statues were placed here to face the ocean, in fact they were meant to look out over a very large village which today is in ruins. The site was restored in 1960 by the American archaeologist William Mulloy. During the restoration, it took a full month—using a stone ramp and two wooden levers—to raise the first of the seven Moai. By the time they got to the last Moai, the same task took them less than a week.

21/ Parting Thoughts

As I tried to state at the beginning, this is in no way a definitive study of Rapa Nui, but is simply an overview. Many books have been written about the island, with some insisting that the Polynesians made everything and were the only inhabitants, while others insist that extraterrestrials had some kind of input.

Most painfully, I believe, are those books which claim they have "solved" all of the riddles, and yet few have ever consulted with the Rapa Nui people themselves, which I find appalling. Having only visited the island twice, I was clearly limited in terms of time access to the Native population, but did my best to glean what I could. One problem that did arise was that different local people gave contradictory information. Whether that was because their sources were dissimilar, or that they were protecting their oral traditions by leading me astray is unclear.

I do plan to visit the island at least once a year, and have an agreement with Hugh Newman of Megalithomania to do so each November. The result of these follow up journeys will lead to changes, for the better I hope, to this book.

An Ahu not listed in the book; I challenge you to find it.

Caves are abundant on the island...

The twinning of Rapa Nui and Paracas Peru in 2012

Where there is light, there is wisdom...

22/ Bibliography

1/ An English translation of the originally Dutch journal by Jacob Roggeveen, with additional significant information from the log by Cornelis Bouwman, was published in: Andrew Sharp (ed.), The Journal of Jacob Roggeveen (Oxford 1970).

2/ William Thompson (1891) Invention of the name "Rapa Nui"

3/ Pinart, Alphonse (in French) (on-line book text) VOYAGE A L'ILE DE PAQUES (OCÉAN PACIFIQUE)

4/ Heyerdahl's view was that the two islands were about the same size, and that "big" and "small" were not physical but historical attributes, "big" indicating the original. In reality, however, Easter Island is more than four times bigger than Rapa Iti. Heyerdahl also stated that there is an island called "Rapa" in Lake Titicaca in South America, but so far there is no map available showing an island of that name in the lake.

5/ Routledge, Katherine. 1919. The Mystery of Easter Island. The story of an expedition. London. Page 201

6/ Heyderdahl, Thor. *Easter Island – The Mystery Solved*. Random House New York 1989.

7/ Donahue, James. http://perdurabo10.tripod.com/galleryg/id49.html

8/ Hunt, T. L.; Lipo, CP (2006). "Late Colonization of Easter Island". *Science* 311 (5767): 1603–6.

9/ An English translation of old logbooks and original letters in connection with both Roggeveen's and Gonzilcs' visits to Easter Island is contained in vol. xm of the Hakluyt Society, Cambridge, England, 1908.

9a/ Øystein Kock Johansen, 'Modus vivendi within Polynesian archaeology in relation to the connection Easter Island – Peru', www.museumsnett.no/kon-tiki/Research/Tucume, part 1.

9b/ John Flenley and Paul Bahn, The Enigmas of Easter Island, New York: Oxford University Press, 2002, p. 58.

9c/ W.R. Corliss (ed.), Anomaly Register, no. 3, October 1997, p. 1.

9d/ Easter Island: The mystery solved, p. 163.

9e/ http://davidpratt.info/easter1.htm

10/ Sarmiento de Gamboa, Pedro 1943. *Historia de los Incas*. Buenos Aires: Emecé Editores.

11/ Foerster, Brien 2010 A Brief History Of The Incas; From Rise, Through Reign To Ruin. CKMV Press, Lima.

12/ http://www.bradshawfoundation.com/thor/kon-tiki.php

13/http://www.personal.psu.edu/pjc12/Easter%20Island%20and%20the%20Ra%20and%20Viracocha%20Expeditions.htm

14/ http://www.bradshawfoundation.com/thor/balsa-raft.php

15/ Personal conversation with Juan Navarro, Paracas History Museum.

16/ Sweet Potato, Consultative Group on International Agricultural Research

17/ "Gardening at the Edge: Documenting the Limits of Tropical Polynesian Kumara Horticulture in Southern New Zealand", University of Canterbury.

18/ Encyclopædia Britannica Online: Lake Titicaca. Retrieved 2007-JUL-12
19/ Fischer, Steven R. *Drought, vegetation change, and human history on Rapa Nui* Reaktion Books, Ma7 2005 ISBN: 978-1861892454 pp.7-8

20/ Øystein Kock Johansen, 'Modus 139ivendi within Polynesian archaeology in relation to the connection Easter Island – Peru', www.museumsnett.no/kon-tiki/Research/Tucume, part 1

21/ West, Barbara A. (2008). *Encyclopedia of the Peoples of Asia and Oceania, Volume 1*. Infobase Publishing. P. 460.

22/ Anita Smith, *An Archaeology of West Polynesian Prehistory*, 2002.

23/ Anita Smith, *An Archaeology of West Polynesian Prehistory*, 2002.

24/ http://www.teara.govt.nz/en/hawaiki/4

25/ Orbell, Margaret. *Hawaiki: a new approach to Māori tradition.* Christchurch: Canterbury University Press, 1991.

26/ Father Sebastian Englert, *Island at the Centre of the World: New light on Easter Island*, London; Robert Hale & Company, 1970, pp. 45-8; *The Enigmas of Easter Island*, pp. 64-5.

27/ Thor Heyerdahl, *Easter Island: The mystery solved*, New York: Random House, 1989, pp. 110-5.

28/ Francis Mazière, *Mysteries of Easter Island*, London: Collins, 1969, pp. 44-5; José Miguel Ramírez and Carlos Huber, *Easter Island: Rapa Nui, a land of rocky dreams*, Alvimpress Impresores, 2000, p. 28.

29/ *Easter Island: The mystery solved*, p. 125.

30/ *Mysteries of Easter Island*, pp. 45, 63

31/ http://davidpratt.info/easter1.htm#e3

32/ http://archive.cyark.org/rapanuiinfo?gclid=CJirn7bxhK0CFQmd7QodpA_boA

32a/ http://davidpratt.info/easter3.htm#e1
32b/ Quoted in Thor Heyerdahl, Easter Island: The mystery solved, New York: Random House, 1989, pp. 230-1.
32c/ John Macmillan Brown, The Riddle of the Pacific, Kempton, IL: Adventures Unlimited, 1996 (1924), p. 1.

33/ Private conversation with Rapa Nui elder, who chose not to be named.

34/ Van Tilburg, Jo Anne. 1994. Easter Island: Archaeology, Ecology and Culture. Washington D.C.: Smithsonian Institution Press. Page 24

35/ http://www.robertschoch.com/sphinxcontent.html

36/ http://www.robertschoch.com/sphinxcontent.html

37/ http://www.ancient-wisdom.co.uk/easterisland.htm

38/ D. Zink. The Ancient Stones Speak. 1979. Musson Publishing

38b/ Routledge, Katherine (1919). *The Mystery of Easter Island. The story of an expedition*. London. ISBN 0-404-14231-1.

39/ http://www.netaxs.com/~trance/annex.html

40/ http://sacredsites.com/americas/chile/easter_island.html

41/ Métraux. A. (1957). Easter Island: A Stone-Age Civilization of the Pacific. London: Andre Deutsch.

41b/ http://www.independent.co.uk/environment/nature/rats-not-men-to-blame-for-death-of-easter-island-431105.html

41c/ http://www.independent.co.uk/environment/nature/rats-not-men-to-blame-for-death-of-easter-island-431105.html

42/ http://www.mysteriousplaces.com/Easter_Island/html/tour3.html

43/ http://www.bradshawfoundation.com/easter/sentinels_in_stone2.php

44/ Easter Island–the mystery solved / Thor Heyerdahl 1989

44b/ David Hatcher Childress, Lost Cities of Ancient Lemuria & the Pacific, Stelle, IL: Adventures Unlimited Press, 1988, pp. 319-20.

44c/ Francis Mazière, Mysteries of Easter Island, London: Collins, 1969, pp. 134-5.

45/ http://www.angelfire.com/tx/wiccanfeatherwood/colors.html

46/ http://www.netaxs.com/~trance/fischer.html

46b/ John Flenley and Paul Bahn, The Enigmas of Easter Island, New York: Oxford University Press, 2002, p. 187.

46c/ Jacques B.M. Guy, 'The Easter Island tablets', www.netaxs.com/~trance/rongo2.html; www.rongorongo.org.
46d/ John Macmillan Brown, The Riddle of the Pacific, Kempton, IL: Adventures Unlimited, 1996 (1924), pp. 52-3, 84.

47/ Thor Heyerdahl. Early Man and the Ocean. 1978. George Allen and Unwin.

48/ Thor Heyerdahl. Early Man and the Ocean. 1978. George Allen and Unwin.

49/ http://www.ancient-wisdom.co.uk/easterisland.htm

50/ http://library.puc.edu/pitcairn/pitcairn/history.shtml

51/ http://en.wikipedia.org/wiki/Ahu_Vinapu

52/ Jean Hervé Daude Île de Pâques – L'empreinte des Incas
53/ John Macmillan Brown, The Riddle of the Pacific, Kempton, IL: Adventures Unlimited, 1996 (1924), p. 1.

54/ Ibid., pp. 257-8.

55/ http://www.bibliotecapleyades.net/arqueologia/eastern_island/easter03.htm

56/ Quoted in Thor Heyerdahl, Easter Island: The mystery solved, New York: Random House, 1989, pp. 230-1.

57/ http://en.wikipedia.org/wiki/Orongo

58/http://www.bradshawfoundation.com/easter/birdman_motif_easter_island.php

59/ The Mystery of Easter Island 1919 - Katherine Routledge ISBN 0-932813-48-8

60/ El Ritual del Hombre-Pajaro – the bird-man cult of Rapa Nui by Bob Gosford

61/ Van Tilburg, J. A. Hoa Hakananai'a (British Museum Press 2004), p.38

62/ "RapaNui Sprache - Übersetzung Buchstabe N"

63/http://chianyong.files.wordpress.com/2011/06/schochbaddeleyeasterislandpropo sal.pdf

63b/ Quoted in John Dos Passos, Easter Island: Island of enigmas, New York: Doubleday, 1971, p. 92.

64/ http://archaeology.about.com/od/rterms/qt/Rano-Raraku.htm

65/ http://archaeology.about.com/od/rterms/qt/Rano-Raraku.htm

66/http://chianyong.files.wordpress.com/2011/06/schochbaddeleyeasterislandpropo sal.pdf

67/ http://www.pbs.org/wgbh/nova/easter/explore/ahutahai.html

68/ http://davidpratt.info/easter3.htm

69/ John Macmillan Brown, The Riddle of the Pacific, Kempton, IL: Adventures Unlimited, 1996 (1924), p. 1.

70/ http://www.mysteriousplaces.com/Easter_Island/html/site5.html

71/ http://www.davidpratt.info/easter3.htm#e1

72/ http://archive.cyark.org/perspective-of-te-pito-kura-navel-of-the-world-taken-from-the-southwest-created-from-laser-scan-data-media

Other Books By Brien Foerster

All of my books are available in e-version through my websites:

www.hiddenincatours.com
www.brienfoerster.com
www.hiddenincavideos.com

As well as:

www.amazon.com

Paperback copies can be found at:

www.lulu.com

Except: **The Enigma Of Cranial Deformation**, co-authored with David Hatcher Childress, which is available through his publishing company:

www.adventuresunlimitedpress.com

CRIMSON HORIZON

The Mysterious Sea Kings
of the Pacific

Brien Foerster

The people of the Pacific known by most as "Polynesians" remain a mystery to scholars and the public alike as to their origins. While most academics in the fields of archaeology and anthropology strongly insist that they exclusively came from south east Asia, other researchers, and the oral traditions of the people themselves often differ with this opinion.

The presence of red hair, called "Ehu" in Hawaii and "Uru Kehu" in some of the ancient and present populations suggest connections, in the distant past, with sea farers from coastal Peru, especially the Paracas, to account for this.

The famous explorer Thor Heyerdahl was insistent that there were ancient connections between Peru and the Pacific Islands, and this book attempts to solve this riddle, without delving into Celtic or other possible European ancestry. Come explore the possibilities through science, wind directions, sea currents, sculpture, and oral traditions.

THE REAL HISTORY OF HAWAII

FROM ORIGINS TO THE END OF THE MONARCHY

BRIEN FOERSTER

The majority of books written about Hawaii, in my experience, contain little information about the Hawaiians themselves, and especially about their history prior to the arrival of Captain James Cook. I lived in Hawaii, and learned the oral traditions from the Hawaiians themselves. Two major waves of migration occurred there, separated by more than 1000 years. And it was the interaction, battles, and melding of these two peoples that make up who the Hawaiians were to become. Where did the Hawaiians come from? What is a Kahuna? Who were the Hawaiian monarchs? And how did the US "acquire" this chain of islands? This book answers these questions, and many more.

LOST ANCIENT TECHNOLOGY
OF PERU & BOLIVIA

BRIEN FOERSTER

Ancient Peru and Bolivia, like Egypt, contain enigmas and mysteries, especially in stone which most conventional scholarship can`t explain. Rather than simply being the exclusively the works of cultures such as the Inca, there are many megalithic wonders which defy both the conventional time lines and known levels of technology attributed to the ancient people of South America. The most glaring example is most likely Puma Punku, near the shore of Lake Titicaca in Bolivia, which hints at not only being several thousand years old, but also seems to have been achieved using what we would call high level machine technology.

There are also many sites in Peru, and especially near the city of Cusco that also show the hall marks of having been made by cultures using technology supposedly not known by cultures such as the Inca.

A massive collection of photographic and and detailed analysis is contained in this book, as well as on site observations by leading engineers.

These two sites, which are in fact two separate ages and constructions in the same area have not been satisfactorily been explained by conventional archaeology. Their claims of them being a maximum of 2000 years old, and having been made by stone age people is ridiculous. This book reveals the facts; Puma punku is at least 15,000 years old, and was a metallurgical plant, as was Tiwanaku. Ancient aliens involved? Buy the book to find out.Brien was featured in a 1 hour Ancient Aliens about these amazing places, along with David Hatcher Childress, Erik von Danniken, George Noory of Coast To Coast AM and Hugh Newman of Megalithomania.

BRIEN FOERSTER
MACHU PICCHU
VIRTUAL GUIDE & SECRETS REVEALED

Machu Picchu is the most popular destination for people visiting Peru. However, many of the guides there are not as well informed as they could be. For example, do they tell visitors that the famous Hitching Post Of The Sun was not made by the Inca, but is actually thousands of years older? Do they know that the original name of Machu Picchu is Yllampu, which means "the dwelling place of the gods?" There are sections of this "Lost City" which are clearly older, as in thousands of years older than the Inca. This little book is a virtual guide to this majestic place; the reader will "walk" step by step from the entrance point and through the whole site, aiding by many colour photographs. And it was written by me, Brien Foerster, who is a professional Machu Picchu guide.

INCA FOOTPRINTS

WALKING TOURS OF CUSCO AND THE SACRED VALLEY OF PERU

BRIEN FOERSTER

Inca Footprints: I wrote this book as the result of not finding anything similar to it in Cusco, or anywhere. Cusco and the Sacred Valley are full of ancient megalithic stone remains and structures, many of which are far older than the Inca, and this fact is not explained, and in fact not known by many of the guides and tour companies there. This book is the result of 5 years of on the ground research by me, Brien Foerster, and contains so many photos, that the book acts as a virtual tour of the whole area.

Printed in Great Britain
by Amazon.co.uk, Ltd.,
Marston Gate.